My Vegan Dreams

A Handbook for a Rational, Responsible Vegan Lifestyle

by

Megan Alpha

WARNING: When discussing the ethical reasons why Veganism is preferable to our standard modern diet, it's impossible not to mention some pretty disgusting things. Sadly, the sheer barbarism of these practices is the strongest argument for adopting Veganism. Animals are fully capable of feeling pain, and most of the ways they are killed for food or their bodily products are inhumane, terrifying, agonizing, and unforgivably slow. Reading about these processes is not for the faint of heart, so I thought I would leave it up to you if you want to avoid the sections where I discuss these awful practices.

So in the text of this book, I will set off the more horrifying discussions with this caution symbol before and after:

If you want to avoid these sections, you can. If you want to add fuel to your reasons for becoming Vegan, don't.

Table of Contents

Introduction: Why We Need a Vegan World

Last year, more than *56 billion* animals in the industrialized world alone were methodically slaughtered to satisfy human hunger. This doesn't even include the animals killed by individuals rather than corporations, whether on family farms, in the jungles of Africa, South America, and coastal Australia as "bush meat" by those who prefer to live off the land or do so for economic reasons, or on the lakes and in the forests of "civilized" nations during the millions of hunting trips taken annually by individuals and groups of friends and family. Not all these animals are killed for food. Many hunted animals end up wasted, with only their skins, scales, horns, or feathers kept as trophies—satisfying a psychological hunger rather than a physical one.

A monumental waste.

At least every single "by-product" of the animals killed in the nauseating, stinking abattoirs of the world is put to some use, whether as dog chewies with cute names or as ground-up animal feed for the next round of animals to be slaughtered. This is how Mad Cow Disease spreads, by the way: slaughterhouses often include brain matter and other tissues of slaughtered cattle in the cow chow they provide to feed lots. We humans learned the danger of this the hard way, in the 1986-98 epidemic that killed dozens of people, mostly in the United Kingdom.

What are these cows eating?

Nothing gets wasted in the livestock industry.

A significant percentage of the animals we deliberately kill every year are literally sacrificed on the altar of style—often for simple raw materials we can easily and cheaply make artificially, like feathers, leather, fur, even claws, teeth, and scales. Have we learned nothing from the wholesale slaughter of the passenger pigeon, whose flocks once darkened the skies of North America with their numbers? Now the species is completely extinct—mostly because their feathers were briefly popular in ladies' hats over a century ago!

A passenger pigeon shoot in Louisiana, 1875

Fur bearing animals are still raised in sordid, unsanitary farms just to be made into coats, gloves, stoles, and hats, especially in the Third World. As if killing them in appalling numbers weren't enough, most aren't killed in humane or even quick ways. That would damage the "product." I'll wait until the appropriate chapter to discuss those ways. Just be prepared to see the following symbol a lot:

Check the first page of this book, before the Table of Contents, to find out what it means if you haven't already.

The much-maligned coyote

We kill some animals just because they're ugly, smelly, or people don't like them. Ranchers often go out of their way to kill skunks, for example, because of their scent defense. Some farmers and home owners in the south kill armadillos because they root around in the ground, leaving unsightly "snout pits" where they were looking for bugs and worms. Some ranchers even go so far as to catch coyotes alive, then wire shut their mouths shut before releasing them, so they'll slowly, helplessly starve to death, their spirits unnecessarily broken. That's just plain evil. A bullet in the head would be more humane.

Many wild animal deaths occur just because they get in the way of something else, with no deliberate attempt at cruelty. Commercial fishermen may be the worst transgressors here. Billions of marine animals are snared as "by-catch" in nets meant for other species. Shrimpers, for example, don't care about most of the fish, horseshoe crabs, jellies, and other marine life they also catch in their nets. They might choose an occasional fish or squid to take home for dinner, or collect a few small species to sell as bait, but usually they throw the rest back into the ocean. Often, it's too late for them to survive: the by-catch animals are dead. That's why clouds of seagulls follow shrimp boats.

A coastal shrimp trawler ready for work

For hundreds of years, tuna fishermen deliberately hacked off the snouts of dolphins, among the most intelligent of animals, with machetes before tossing them back into the oceans to starve to death. Even today, sword fishermen, who hate blue sharks with a passion (because they're mostly what they catch), play "football" with them and otherwise deliberately kill or maim them. Asian fishermen chop the fins off sharks for shark-fin soup—and then throw the mortally injured fish back into the water, where they are soon killed or die. This practice has recently immigrated to the New World.

Nothing goes to waste in the ocean, but those are shockingly cold reasons to kill an animal. It should come as no surprise that the more "desirable" species of shark are now endangered. In many nations, recreational fishermen are no longer allowed to catch sharks, or have very stringent limits. In my home state of Texas, for example, you can only legally keep one shark a day, and it must be at least two feet long.

And that's not even the worst of it. In many parts of the world, superstition STILL "requires" the murder of thousands of increasingly rare animals like wild salmon, tigers, bears, wolves, rhinos, lions, and whales for traditional medicinal purposes... or disgustingly, to act as so-called aphrodisiacs for people with too much money who ought to know better. In this era, we KNOW that magic doesn't work. So why do so many people still believe in it?

No, you *don't* need the gall bladder of a tiger or powdered rhino horn that costs thousands of dollars to cure you of some obscure ailment that has never been diagnosed by a licensed medical professional. In this era, when we've proven the value of science billions of times in thousands of ways, hanging onto superstitions that require the sacrifice of any form of life is no less than a sin. It's a mortal sin when that superstition requires the life of an animal already on the brink of extinction.

The Sumatran tiger, a species endangered by superstition

The Moral Reality

Killing animals for their meat and other products is NOT NECESSARY in the modern world. Plain and simple. Not. Necessary. It doesn't matter how many times critics of vegetarianism and Veganism invoke the human need for protein and fats to stay healthy, this remains true. There are plenty of plant-based proteins and fats to feed the entire world in a healthy fashion many times over.

Thousands of years ago, there may have been a need for people to feed off animal flesh, especially in places like the Arctic, where plants are rare for most of the year. In fact, some groups of pure Eskimo (Inuit and Aleut peoples) require an enzyme found in meat to survive, probably because of their diets, which once consisted almost entirely of meat products. But today, that need can be met by modern medicine for those few who actually need it. All it takes is a few pills a week.

Interestingly, historical accounts of Eskimo life tell us that they *craved* plant foods. They ate vegetation whenever they could get it—even when they found it in the stomach of an animal they had just killed! Some tundra animals, like the ubiquitous caribou that was a staple of the native Alaskan diet until recently, have a talent for finding hidden vegetation even in the dead of winter. The Eskimos considered the partially digested plants a delicacy, as well they might. They needed the vitamins plants contain, nutrients that are rare in animal flesh.

If you look at the artifacts left behind by most ancient cultures, you might conclude that they were mostly hunters, and that meat made up most of their diets. Some archaeologists and anthropologists cling hard to this viewpoint. But think about it: what materials survive longest in the ground? Stone and bone. Stone, in fact, survives almost untouched. And what tools were made of stone and bone? Mostly weapons, and tools for killing, skinning, and defleshing animals. Later cultures might have had a little metal, which can also survive a long time. But here's the thing: Every culture, even ours, has a lot of tools made of wood, natural fibers, and other plant products. They wouldn't survive very long even if there were a lot of them, except sometimes in a very dry or very wet environment.

The truth is that the "big game hunters" probably survived mostly on plant foods and smaller animals, only occasionally gorging on meat from big game like mammoths and bison. Men were the hunters, so where did most of the plant foods come from? The efforts of the women. Sometimes, we see evidence of the plant foods exploited from seeds or fibers preserved in fire pits, or in coprolites (dried dung). Later, after most of the largest land animals like mastodons and mammoths died out (possibly with human help) we see the rise of stone grinding tools. These became especially common as people started to settle down and farm. Well-used grinding tools like manos and metates became very common.

A stone mano and metate, tools used for grinding grains and seeds

Ancient people ate meat when they could get it because they needed to, and didn't know better. Even hundreds of years ago, most people didn't know better. They killed and ate livestock because it was what they thought food was, even when it would have been more logical to eat plants. When these cultures ate a primarily vegetarian diet, it was because they had to. The Irish of the 1840s are a good example. Because of harsh English policies not allowing them to raise cattle on common lands or poach the deer brought in for the aristocracy, the Irish ate a lot of potatoes, and grew almost nothing else, probably because potatoes took well to Irish soils and were easy to grow. When the potatoes contracted a blight, the Irish people starved in their millions. Many came to America for a better life, and found it.

We are not our ancestors. We now know, through undebatable scientific fact, that *human beings don't have to eat meat to stay healthy*, not if we're practical and careful. One of the best qualities of our species is that we humans are so adaptable. Like so many adaptable animals, we can survive by eating just about anything, including an all-vegetable diet.

Margarine works just fine, thanks

We can also make the conscious decision to use no resources or materials that derive from exploiting animals, even things that don't really hurt the animal: not wool, not milk, not cast-off antlers or horns, nothing. Every product we need we can make artificially, often from plant materials, even the things we've traditionally gotten from animals—and usually the "fakes" are tougher and last longer.

Cheese can be made from nuts. Similarly, milk can be made from soy or almonds, and it tastes just as good on your bran flakes as cow juice. Even plastics, which are often made from petroleum—the remains of dinosaurs and other animals and plants millions of years dead—can be made from plant products like sawdust, and believe it or not, companies are now experimenting with marketing plastics made from airborne pollutants—literally from thin air!

All it takes is a little research, and maybe going out of your way a little, to find what you need. But *it's not that hard*, especially with the world of knowledge and resources we know as the Internet. And I believe we have a moral obligation to move from a meat-based diet to one that's completely plant-based.

Look: The simple reality is that no one in the modern world has to eat animal products, except *maybe* in dire life-or-death emergencies. Most people eat animal products out of habit, or because they like to. But you don't *have* to. There's nothing in animal products that you can't get from plants. Even if you have some metabolic deficiency that you can control by eating meat, all you have to do is take dietary supplements instead. Very few, if any, are so expensive the average person can't afford them.

Undermining Our Own Evolution

Although there have been some setbacks and mistakes that took us temporarily down the wrong path, the cultural and biological history of humanity has been generally progressive, from unwitting barbarism toward greater enlightenment. A thousand years ago, otherwise good people wouldn't have thought twice about murdering someone in cold blood just because they belonged to another religion. This still happens, but it's almost universally condemned among right-thinking people.

Two hundred years ago, most Americans, even our Founding Fathers, didn't think twice about the morality of owning other people. The enlightened ancient Greeks and Romans did it, after all. Colonial Americans sometimes didn't even consider their African- and Indian-descended slaves people, just because their skins were a different color. That's as stupid now as thinking eye color matters when it comes to ability or intelligence. It's just a genetic variation, nothing more. And ironically, the Land of the Free was one of the last industrialized countries on earth to abolish chattel slavery. Today, the very thought is universally abhorrent.

Two decades ago, the idea that people of the same sex could get married and have all the benefits of a traditional marriage was almost unthinkable. Yet in July 2015, the U.S. Supreme Court made same-sex marriage legal, with all the rights allowed heterosexual marriage, in all 50 states and the various territories we govern—and the negative response was underwhelming. Most people, despite a number of hard-fought legal challenges by what turned out to be a very vocal but small minority, cheered the Court's ruling or quietly accepted it. While there remain some diehard holdouts, they're relatively few.

Other countries went this route years ago, and civil society has yet to collapse. If anything, things have improved for most of us.

Like the poor, cultural "Neanderthals" will always be with us. But despite them, the human race is gradually evolving into something better: a more moral, tolerant, and technologically sophisticated species. But we still have a long way to go. There are still barbarous practices we have to eliminate from our society if we expect to continue to evolve toward a better destiny.

Eating meat is one of them.

No, let me correct that: eating meat itself is not actually the problem. If hamburgers and hotdogs grew on trees and ripened like bananas before being picked, that would probably be acceptable. There would be no pain and suffering involved. The *real* problem is how we obtain the meat. There's no way around the fact that we have to slaughter animals to get the meat so popular to our lifestyles. That's bad enough. Even worse is the way we do it. Even if the process were painless and more humane, intentionally taking a life is unacceptable. But the way livestock is raised and slaughtered is unnecessary vicious – as I will discuss in detail in a later chapter. Some practices are particularly heartbreaking. Did you know, for example, that "strangled duck" is considered a delicacy by gourmets? That's right. Someone *strangles a duck* to death before they dress it, press out the blood and other juices to mix with cognac, and then cook the mixture to make a "sizzling red sauce." The historic 435-year-old restaurant *La Tour d'Argent* in Paris is famous for it; as of 2003, they had served 1 million of them in the previous century. They press the duck right there in the restaurant, in full view of the diners, and even include a postcard with the cooked animal to indicate its "serial number." According to Wikipedia (admittedly not the best authority ever), "Serial number #112,151 went to U.S. President Franklin Delano Roosevelt, #203,728 went to Marlene Dietrich, and #253,652 went to Charlie Chaplin."

Whatever the serial number, they charge about 70 Euros for the privilege of buying and eating half a strangled, pressed, and numbered duck for lunch.

Can't people see that killing animals in ways like this, and, worse, taking pleasure and pride in it, undermines our social evolution? Why don't they *care*? The fact that all the non-vegetarians and non-Vegans out there who aren't directly involved in the slaughter trade just close their eyes to it and let it happen is nearly as bad. Writer Hannah Arendt coined the phrase "banality of evil" when discussing Adolf Eichmann, one of Adolf Hitler's top lieutenants, and the way that the German, Polish, and Austrian peoples closed their eyes to the murder of more than 11 million men, women, and children in Nazi concentration camps during World War II. They had to know that Jews, Gypsies, the mentally ill, and the other "undesirables" herded into those crowded camps were being systematically worked to death, starved to death, or just outright murdered. The fact that they went in and never came out should have told been a huge clue. The clouds of evil-smelling smoke from the incinerators. The fields of turned earth stained red. But they closed their eyes to it.

I'm not saying that animal lives are more valuable than human lives; I would never argue that. Nor do I believe that invoking Nazis here invalidates my arguments, as some cocky debaters might argue. Slaughterhouses and feedlots are basically animal concentration camps, no matter how we dress them up or work to consider them otherwise.

A duck press, used for squeezing bodily fluids out of strangled ducks.

What I *am* saying is that all animal life is precious. These lives are sacred. It's not our right or our privilege to end them. Human beings are not gods. Nor are we animals, with no choice but to kill to survive. We can use our culture, our intelligence, our opposable thumbs, our technological prowess to find other ways to survive, other foods to live on. It's not as if plant foods taste bad, or they're so bland we can hardly stand them. They're bursting with flavor. Spices—nearly all of which are plant-based, incidentally—just improve that flavor. Plants, which turn sunlight into food and carbon dioxide into breathable oxygen, *ultimately support all life on Earth.* They are the real staff of life, and have been for many thousands of years, since long before recorded history. If God created *anything* for us to assert dominance over, it was these miraculous living things: mindless life forms with no central nervous systems that stay constantly in one place their entire lives, and in many, many cases, deliberately produce fruits and grains MEANT to be eaten by animals, so their seeds will be scattered far and wide and fertilized in the process by what just may be the very best fertilizer nature makes: animal dung! It's a perfect system, easy to take advantage of, and it's found almost everywhere—even in the polar deserts of Antarctica.

So why are we staining our souls by killing, or allowing to be killed, tens of billions of lives per year? Why are we crushing our own morality by torturing most of those animals during their short, sad lives?

An Important Aside

One of the sad realities of life is that for you to live, other beings must die. I accept that. But there are limits.

I know that I, and you, and everyone in this world, inadvertently ends the lives of hundreds or thousands of small living beings every day, from microbes to insects. Even if we sat in one place and didn't move a muscle, we'd probably still be responsible for little deaths like these. They are inevitable. There are people who try to avoid such things; the Jains of India actually carry brooms everywhere they go, to sweep the ground clean of insects so they don't step on them. Most of us don't and can't go this far. We just have to try to cause as little damage as possible.

I'm fully aware that plants must die so that I can eat. All Vegans are. Some of us try to avoid this by subsisting only on plant foods that the plants willingly let go of: windblown fruits, ripe grains, and the like. That is, after all, their ultimate

15

purpose. But such foods are hard to obtain, especially most of the year, so it's a hungry and unsustainable existence.

We all have to eat. There has to be a cut-off point. Again, let me point out that plants lack a central nervous system. They can't feel pain, so I feel no shame in eating harvested plant foods, which are often impossible to obtain without killing all or part of the plant. I'm telling you this as a foil to critics who claim I'm being hypocritical, since I too eat things that were killed. But I don't eat things that move, have beating hearts, or faces. My food sources are sustainable, healthy, good for me, good for my soul, good for the earth, and good for society.

That's how I answer such critics.

Here's the long and the short of it, okay? **In the modern world, eating meat is not necessary.** It supports an inhumane livestock industry that undermines our ethical evolution. It also supports the systematic exploitation of limited marine resources that, despite the vastness of the sea, is not a sustainable practice! Don't believe me? Two hundred years ago, cod were so numerous you could barely wet a hook without catching one. They were so common most people wouldn't eat them. They were considered good enough only for slaves or the poor. Same goes for lobsters; there are documented cases where criminals in penitentiaries near the ocean considered having to eat lobster every day to be cruel and unusual punishment. Repeatedly, commercial fishermen have depleted one species to the point they had to turn to another for their livelihood. Cod, salmon, orange roughy, mahi-mahi, pollock, flounder... one after the other. Is it any wonder that the most common fishes on restaurant menus are now farm-raised catfish and tilapia?

Livestock raising and commercial fishing has other negative environmental impacts. Raising livestock takes land out of rotation that could be used for more intensive food production, and animal wastes pollute our land and water supplies. There was a time when chicken plantations in the Southern U.S. thought nothing of dumping offal—guts, feathers, feet, and heads—into local streams. Now it's too valuable as animal feed and for processing into, believe it or

16

not, crude oil. Still awful and not good for the Earth, but arguably more sustainable. And this doesn't even touch on the massive amounts of liquid and solid waste that too many animals in too close proximity produce, which yield misery, horrible odors that sicken locals, and encourage the spread of disease.

All in all, meat production as it exists today is wasteful, dangerous, and terrible for the Earth. In the chapters to come, I'm going to discuss in great detail why we need a Vegan world.

Who Am I to Tell You All This?

As of mid-2016, I'm an 18-year-old who has been fully committed to the Vegan lifestyle for nearly two years. I made the decision to go Vegan back in August 2014, when my mother and I were on a family vacation in New Hampshire. We had just finished eating dinner, and something weird occurred to me. People were devouring their meals and commenting openly about how amazing the lobster, the fish, and the beef tasted... and for some reason I started thinking about the animals whose flesh I was consuming. I wondered whether I should become Vegan to protect animals, and became disgusted as I thought about the creatures that had given their lives so that we could all sit in a nice restaurant and eat their flesh, with barely a second thought for what they had sacrificed. Which was literally everything.

I had just turned 16. That night, Mom and I started to seriously research how lobsters were caught and killed—and I was horrified. I watched video after video of how lobsters were caught, and the process they went through going from the sea to your plate. I had no idea until then that their entire bodies were made up of nerves—and they could feel *everything*. Think about how we cook lobsters: we literally boil them alive. Can you imagine a more painful death? And *why* do we boil them alive? Because if they don't die until we cook them, then they're fresher... and they provide that wonderful taste my fellow diners were remarking about in the restaurant.

One of the crustaceans that changed my life

I was sickened. I thought about how selfish I was for killing a living being, just to satisfy my taste buds. That led me to watch videos on the process of how chickens, cows, lambs, fish, pigs, ducks, buffalo, calves, and eggs made it to our dinner plates. I was utterly horrified. I realized at that very moment I could no longer participate in such cruelty to animals.

I went Vegan cold turkey with my mother that very night—right in the middle of my vacation, in lobster heaven, probably the seafood capital of the world. We got home back to Dallas, committed to the lifestyle, and have never broken our commitment. I will admit that it did take a month or so to really educate myself on what Veganism is and what it is not when it comes to prepared meals and eating out. Nowadays, being Vegan is easy for me. It's not only about what I put *in* my body, but also what I put *on* my body. It's not just about being not eating meat for me. It's a lifestyle.

My goal and mission in life now is to inspire and educate young and old on how to become Vegan, and how to deal with the issues that arise from being Vegan—such as what to eat when you go out to dinner, how to deal with unsupportive family members, how to respond to questions people ask about being Vegan, and much, much more. I want to be a voice for the animals who don't have a voice.

It's my dream that one day, the majority of our society will realize that Vegan is the way to go. It's good for you, good for the environment, and most of all, it's good for the animals.

Here's the way I see it. Many people are meat-eaters and animal exploiters out of habit. The don't know any better, any more than I did before I had my epiphany in that New Hampshire restaurant. They haven't thought much about the misery and suffering that brings the meat to their table: not just the suffering by the animals that meat used to be, but also the suffering of our planet, and ultimately of our entire species, both physically and morally. They don't know that there are perfectly healthy, economical, plant-based alternatives to every meat product. Nor do they realize that we don't have to exploit animals for fur, wool, milk, or any other renewable resource. Plants and other materials, even things we previously thought of as pollution, can provide it all.

My goal is to teach whoever cares to listen about what they can do to become Vegan, and live lives more responsible not just to themselves, but to the world and the universe at large. That may sound a bit high-minded, but I have great confidence in the human race. I know that we can become so much better than what we have been in the past.

Core values define who we are as people, and ultimately what we become. They also underlie the Mission and Vision of our lives. Just like the Mission and Vision of a corporation, these three things guide what we do and how we see the world. I believe that by abandoning the exploitation of other animals, be they crustacean, reptile, or mammal, we will better ourselves and our world. This is my way of fighting for what I believe is right, and taking my message to everyone. At least a third of the world is connected electronically, with more to come in the near future. The audience is a large one; and, I believe, it's ready to embrace the Vegan cause, if given enough reason.

My Platforms

I'm a passionate person when it comes to my beliefs and core values, including Veganism. So, when I returned home from that fateful vacation, I set out to shout my message to the world. I know that I'm not the only one out there promoting the Vegan message, but I also knew that there was always room for one more person to help spread the news—and that if I could convince just a few people to stop exploiting animals, I'd put our species that much closer to our ethical maturity. Ultimately, I want to educate as many people as I can, all around the world; I have an advantage, a pulpit if you will, that many of my fellow Vegans do not. Because I belong to a family of successful, tech-savvy entrepreneurs, I knew how to best broadcast my message in this era of the Internet, Facebook, and information that yearns to be free. Even though I was just 16 at the time, I knew I could make a difference... and I have.

Already, my younger sister has become a pescatarian (that is, the only meat she eats is fish), partly because she saw an episode of *Survivor* in which the people on the island killed a chicken for dinner. My father is well on his way to the Vegan lifestyle, too. And with my parents' help, I was able to set up several successful platforms from which I could spread my message with everything from blogs to Vegan food reviews to collections of tasty pure Vegan recipes.

My main platform is my website, not coincidentally called My Vegan Dreams. You can find it at **MyVeganDreams.com**. That's where I post most of my content, which I do on a regular basis. Not only do I post blogs, I also do vlogs —video blogs—that I post on my YouTube Channel. And then there's my Facebook page and Instagram page also called My Vegan Dreams, which I invite people to join on a regular basis, especially when they comment on my website. I'm always looking for intelligent discussions about the Vegan lifestyle, and while I do try to promote my own Vegan agenda, I don't condemn anyone else for their diets or beliefs. The truth is, *I'm* more likely to be criticized! Some people practically equate Veganism with atheism or communism, and they're pretty vocal about it, at least through the anonymity of the Internet. But that's okay—they have their freedom of speech, and I have mine.

Ironically, when some people see someone promoting Veganism, they react as if I'm trying to take away their freedom to eat meat. I'm not. I would love for them to change their minds voluntarily, but forcing the change—even if I had that power—would be against the very principles of freedom I believe in.

But I know that I and people like me are making a difference. I'm proud to say that I've had hundreds of thousands of unique hits on My Vegan Dreams, and as of this writing, I've gotten almost 170,000 likes on Facebook and 20,400 followers on Instagram, so I can't complain. The response has been overwhelmingly positive so far, despite some negative responses... and a few weird ones, like the guy who said he was going to stop eating animals and eat Vegans instead! But I have high numbers of followers who are active and committed, so I feel like I'm making headway.

I invite you to join me in the crusade!

Chapter 1: What Veganism Is and Is Not

If you haven't already gotten the point from reading the introduction, Veganism isn't just a diet. It's a lifestyle. Despite what many people think, Veganism is NOT just vegetarianism. There are many reasons for being a vegetarian, and they don't always line up with the reasons for becoming a Vegan. Though a vegetarian diet is a step in the direction of Veganism, people's reasons for it don't always have anything to do with their sympathy for animals. Some people, like Jains, some Hindus, and some Buddhists, are vegetarian for religious reasons only. Some vegetarians avoid meat for health reasons. Some avoid it because they just don't like the taste. I've also heard of people who went through periods (such as in college) when they couldn't afford to eat meat, and by the time they got to a point where they could, their bodies could no longer tolerate animal products. They had completely adjusted to the vegetarian diet—another argument for Veganism.

In this chapter, we'll take a closer look at what distinguishes vegetarianism from Veganism. Note that I always capitalize Vegan, Veganism, and related words in this book. I believe it's that important.

The Big Difference Between Vegetarians and Vegans

When you get right down to it, vegetarianism is just a choice of diet. It's only about what you put into your body. Veganism is more hardcore, affecting your life at ALL levels. It's an ethical choice, a lifestyle in which you strive to avoid all animal products, whether their production hurts the animal or not... and even with some of those, like wool and milk production, the claims of a lack of harm are debatable, or just plain ingenuous. Ultimately, Veganism means USING NO ANIMAL PRODUCTS AT ALL, even those cast off without harm, like deer antlers or shed hair. All of these things can be replaced with other products, artificial or plant-based. Some Vegans even avoid petroleum products, since crude oil originated millions of years ago from decayed organic matter, which may include animals. I'm not sure I would go that far, since whatever animals the petroleum products originated from have been dead for geological epochs, and can hardly be said to be exploited. That would make riding a bus or in a car, or using some lotions and petroleum jelly, completely un-Vegan!

Is an electric car like this Tesla the only acceptable ride? That's up to you

Listen to what your heart tells you in cases like this. Your form of Veganism doesn't have to be extreme, and it especially doesn't have to be militant. Like most Vegans of all types, I get a lot of flak from non-Vegans, but I don't give it. You can encourage Veganism without preaching or being rude, and you definitely don't have to lower yourself to the level of those who, for whatever reason, dislike or even hate the Vegan lifestyle, and don't mind letting you know about it.

Stepping Stones

Earlier, I mentioned that vegetarianism, while not equal to Veganism, is a step in the right direction. And it really is, in any of its forms. Once you've begun to go vegetarian, and you become comfortable with it, it's easy to transition to the next step. Eventually, you'll have no problem moving on to pure Veganism. All it requires is a willingness to change your mindset, and to keep an eagle eye on the things you eat and use to make sure they don't use animal products or exploit animals in any way. This includes beauty products, by the way, which are often tested on lab animals. Animals often have hairspray and other products blasted into their eyes or open wounds to see what will happen, or their hair shaved and their skin slathered with shampoo, conditioner, mascara and other makeup to see if it makes them break out.

But let's leave that discussion for another time, and look at the various types of vegetarian, how they differ from Vegans, and what they have to do to move forward in their efforts to morally evolve and improve the planet, the species, and themselves. My intent is not to preach, but to inform. However, I won't be sad if you decide to up your ante closer to Veganism after reading this, or even go All In!

We'll start with the most basic forms of vegetarian, and move on to the next highest until we discuss pure vegetarianism and Veganism.

The Semi-Vegetarian

Semi-vegetarians are people who are working their way up to vegetarianism. They've cut back on their consumption of animal products significantly, but aren't there yet. Some people split them into a lot of different types, like the pollo-vegetarian, who has cut out red meat altogether and limits their meat-eating to poultry. Pesco-pollo-vegetarians eat poultry and fish. Really, this category is almost infinitely divisible, so it's better just to say "semi-vegetarian."

The Pescatarian

Pescatarians avoid all meats except fish and related marine life, including shellfish (lobsters, crabs, crawfish, shrimp, and prawns), and mollusks (clams, oysters, etc.). It can be argued that most of these animals have very primitive nervous systems and don't really feel pain as such. That's what I thought too until I found out that lobsters are basically just bundles of nerves, as I pointed out earlier. If you've ever seen a boiled lobster or crawfish, you'll notice their tails are tightly curled. That is a pain reaction. The animal was boiled alive. People who love seafood won't even eat a crawfish or lobster that has an uncurled tail, because that means it was dead when it was cooked—and so the meat might not be as flavorful.

Lacto-Ovo Vegetarians

Lacto-ovo vegetarians still eat dairy products and eggs, but otherwise focus on plant foods. A lacto-vegetarian eats dairy products but no eggs. At first glance, this doesn't seem so bad, and sure, it's better than the other forms of vegetarianism. But it's not completely without fault. Until relatively recently, the only way to make cheese was to use a piece of calf stomach called rennet, which contained the right enzymes to make cheese curdle properly. So aside from all the negatives associated with dairy farming (which I will go into in another chapter), calves were killed for the enzymes. Now we can make the enzymes artificially, which eases some people's consciences. However, that still leaves the horror of dairy farming to deal with.

Ovo-vegetarians eat eggs. Eggs are no big deal, right? Well, one of the funniest and scariest comics I ever saw was an old *Far Side* strip showing a farmer's wife leaving the henhouse carrying a basket of eggs... as the hens were leaving her house carrying her baby. It drove home to me the fact that eggs are unborn chickens (or ducks, or geese, or whatever). Every egg eaten is a potential life taken. Often, ovo-vegetarians will eat only eggs from free-range chickens, which ensures that their food doesn't come from animals that were cooped up in tiny cages under 24-hour lights, and fed hormones so they would produce egg after egg. Again, that's a step in the right direction.

Full Vegetarians

According to the Vegetarian Society, a vegetarian is defined as "someone who lives on a diet of grains, nuts, seeds, vegetables and fruits with, or without, the use of dairy products and eggs. A vegetarian does not eat any meat, poultry, game, fish, shellfish or by-products of slaughter." I would say that a full-fledged vegetarian is someone who also avoids dairy products and eggs. They survive only on a diet of plant foods, which isn't as difficult as you might think. There are always alternatives to meat, and with the rise of the Internet, it's easier than ever to find not just the proper foods but the support you need to embrace this liberating lifestyle. From this point, it's an easy step to the next level of the meat-free lifestyle: Veganism.

Vegans

By now, I've probably already made pretty clear what a Vegan is and does. We not only avoid all meats, but also all animal products: so no leather, feathers, horn, bone, ivory, hair of any type including wool, and of course no dairy or egg products, by-products, or anything remotely produced by an animal (except maybe for processed manure when used as compost for growing plants). The only real exception—and some Vegans have a problem with this as well!—is nursing infants with mother's milk. If you're a breastfeeding Vegan mom, just be sure that your diet is complete and especially contains Vitamins A and B12, because the ONLY nourishment a nursing baby gets comes from you—and if you suffer from any nutritional deficiencies, so will your baby. This can endanger the child's health, even if you feel fine.

A perfectly natural process

I see nursing a child as more of a voluntary thing done by the mother for the child's good health. It's perfectly natural; no right-thinking Vegan would condemn a lamb for drinking its own mother's milk, after all. For me, the idea here is to free all *animals* from exploitation. True Vegans do not "harvest" or use products from animals even when they die a natural death. The only biological materials we make use of are made from plant fibers or parts. We have to survive in some way, after all! As I've already argued, plants have no central nervous systems, and thus cannot feel pain. Furthermore, the plant world is diverse enough to provide us with every nutrient we will ever need, as long as we live a normal, healthy lifestyle. Even Vitamin D, which is hard to get without drinking fortified milk these days, comes in pill form. Even better, if you get as little as ten minutes of sun per day, your skin will manufacture Vitamin D from cholesterol.

Now, there's a great way to keep your cholesterol down—a double dose of good health!

Believe it or not, there are also levels of Veganism. It depends on how dedicated you are and what you believe you ought to do to help yourself and the world. Some people, for example, prefer to focus on raw foods only, because they consider it more natural. They believe it preserves the nutritional value of the food, and in fact it often does, according to nutritionists. Some Vegans avoid cooking their food because it saves energy, and the more energy saved, the less damage to the environment. I know a girl who is a "raw Vegan," and will only eat foods heated to less than 140° F. I'm not sure of her reasoning, but as far as preservation goes, she can only eat only sun-dried foods. As you might imagine, this is very limiting and can make for a hungry existence.

Speaking of limiting: some Vegans will eat only food that has fallen from the parent plant, like windblown fruit and grains. Among those who practice this are some Pagans and modern Wicca, who undergo periods when they can't eat any food that has been picked living from a plant, for religious reasons. I've heard that this is a very hungry time for most of them, because such foods tend to be available only for part of the year, and it's rare to find fallen fruit that isn't over-ripe. Tree nuts are much easier to deal with. Personally, I see no need for such extreme Veganism. As I outlined in the introduction, the whole point of most plants having flowers, fruits, nuts, berries, and the like is, first, to attract insects and small animals to help pollinate the plants, then later to attract animals to eat the produce and spread the seeds far and wide in their travels. They're designed by nature to be eaten before they become overripe, so why not pick them? Admittedly, we've redesigned many of them through millennia of breeding to better fit our needs, but the argument still holds.

The truth is, I'm here to save the animals. I might treat Veganism as a kind of religion, but never to the point where I would worship plants. My family has a garden, and we grow a bunch of our own food. There's nothing quite like working with the soil, and it's great to watch our food grow, knowing exactly where it comes from—and that it's fresh and natural, and that growing it ourselves decreases the need to spend resources to travel and buy food. That decreases our carbon footprint, which is always a good thing. Personally, I prefer organic, non-GMO foods that haven't been tampered with or poisoned with chemicals in order to maximize production. You can find food from organic-certified farms without much trouble if you look for it.

The Difficulties of Veganism

Veganism is not for the timid! Even in the modern, highly connected world, you have to struggle sometimes to find the right foods. This is hardest to guarantee in restaurants. Animal products are present even in products you might ordinarily think were completely Vegan. Refried beans and Spanish rice, two staples of Tex-Mex food, are cooked with lard—pig fat. It's especially difficult to eat in restaurants, because unless the place deliberately caters to Vegans, you're going to have a hard time finding Vegan-friendly foods without asking a lot of questions.

A lot of times, the people working in the restaurants aren't at all sympathetic, or just don't understand the Vegan's viewpoint. I've even had a waiter say, "Here's your bunny food," as he handed me my salad, after I explained we were Vegans. You can bet he didn't get a tip from us!

Luckily, once you identify a specific Vegan or vegetarian restaurant, you can keep going there. I have a favorite Vegan bakery, a favorite Vegan restaurant, and a favorite sushi restaurant that makes us Vegan rolls. I love going to California, especially San Francisco and Los Angeles, because restaurants there often cater to Vegans; you usually just have to ask. They're very accommodating, and the chefs will be happy to specially prepare things for you when you're in nice restaurants. And I don't mean just salads, either. Does eating Vegan cost more than eating the standard diet in most restaurants and store- foods? Of course, but really not that much. Anyway, it's worth it, from health, moral, and environmental standpoints alike.

More difficult than finding the right food is dealing with the haters. Now, I'm not one of those Vegans who "witnesses" to other people, telling them how awful they are for eating animals. I'm not militant at all. I've made my decision to be Vegan, and it's one I intend to stick with. I can't make their decisions for others, and that's not my place anyway. I *will* discuss the benefits of Veganism with anyone who asks, but I don't get radical about it. But I still have to deal with people like the "bunny food" waiter, who was on the mild end of the spectrum, to the person in a cafeteria who insulted me by saying that what I'm doing is really wrong, something I still don't understand. Usually, I try not to respond to the haters, but I got mad with this one because they were so hardheaded and refused to listen to me. I'm not entirely passive, but I do tend to be peaceful. I try not to start any fights with anyone about things like this; I explain the truth, and only the truth.

You're going to learn a lot of hard truths in Chapter 3 about the livestock industry, especially factory farming, some of them disgusting.

Thank goodness we live in the digital age, because all these problems of finding food and dealing with haters can be overcome! The Internet has made finding the right food products so much easier. Not only can you order Vegan snack packs and find great menus on the 'Net, you can download apps for both computer and phone that will show you where Vegan-friendly or pure Vegan restaurants are in your area. Every day, people are finding more ways to fill empty marketing niches, and they've finally realized what a rich vein Veganism can be. Ten years ago, it could be very hard to find the right restaurants and stores for our needs. Now it's a snap.

Vegan Guilt

There's one other serious issue that I believe I should address, and that's the factor of Vegan guilt. Of course, we don't feel guilty for eating plants, but very few of us are born to the Vegan lifestyle (though this is slowly changing). In the comments on my Facebook Wall and websites, I sometimes see Vegan converts expressing their guilt and horror that they participated, however distantly or unsuspectingly, in the murder of animals during their meat-eating past. I can understand where they're coming from. However, while it's not my place to tell someone how to feel, I believe that just by going Vegan, you have begun expiating that guilt. No longer will you take part in the animal deaths that are part and parcel of the meat-eating experience.

In my opinion, taking up this enlightened lifestyle makes up for a lot. I believe you can forgive yourself for your past eating habits, because you probably didn't know better, especially when you were a kid. If you feel the need to make up for it, adopt a pet or donate to a charity to help animals, or work with me and others to promote Veganism around the world. The more people who help, the quicker we can end this senseless slaughter and move forward to a better world.

Is Veganism Just for Humans?

This is a good question, and it's always better asked than wondered about —or worse, ignored. Sometimes Vegans make the decision for their pets, usually cats and dogs, to become Vegan as well. Sometimes it works, and sometimes it goes horribly wrong. Check with your veterinarian before shifting your pet's diet to purely Vegan foods, especially if you have an exotic pet such as a ferret or a raptor (a hawk, eagle, or the like) which tend to be carnivorous. Most other birds and rodents are natural herbivores, but by no means all. I've even heard of squirrels, the classic nut-eating rodent, eating baby birds when given the opportunity.

Can your dog be a Vegan? Actually, yes! Although dogs are now recognized as a subspecies of the gray wolf, rather than a separate species of canine (yes, even the tiniest teacup Yorkies and Poms!), they belong to a branch that can digest starches—probably because they've lived with us humans for so long. Wild wolves are what scientists call "obligate carnivores," which means they have no choice but to eat meat in order to survive. Plant foods make them sick, and they can't digest them.

But somewhere, thousands of years ago, one or two groups of wolves (the evidence isn't clear) probably started eating from human trash heaps outside villages. While there were bones and other animal remains there, most of the food scraps would have been plant-based. Through pure luck in the genetic lottery, a few of the wolves had genes for an enzyme called *amylase* that lets them digest starches. These wolves were able to eat plant foods and remain healthy, and as a result, left more descendants than the local wolves that didn't. Eventually, these wolves were tamed by humans, and gradually evolved into the dogs we know today.

The fact is, most dog food is made of corn and similar plant products anyway, with at most a splash of meat or meat flavoring. You can find entirely non-meat dog food, or make it yourself if you're skillful in the kitchen. Many dogs will even eat their vegetables straight. While I don't know many dogs who like fresh leafy greens (at least without salad dressing), most of them love potatoes, baked goods, green beans, asparagus, Brussels sprouts, broccoli, and the like, as long as it's cooked—as many a little kid who doesn't want to eat his vegetables has learned.

So how about your cat? No dice there. Although most dry cat food does have a lot of vegetable materials in it, cats are still obligate carnivores. If they don't get certain enzymes available only in meats, they will die. Of course, there's the possibility that we'll have the artificial enzymes we need to keep them healthy in the future, but until then, you'll just have to hold your nose when feeding your cats "gooshyfood," as one web-cartoonist from Dallas calls it, or not keep cats at all for now.

Your little house wolf can go Vegan with you, but not your cat!

Chapter 2: Health Arguments for Veganism

Human beings are endlessly adaptable. That's probably why we're the dominant species on the planet right now, at least in terms of technology. While insects outnumber us in numbers and weight, we're certainly the most numerous large species ever to live on the planet (as far as we know).

It's interesting, then, that a lot of biologists consider humans to be "primitive" or "generalized", at least from a biological standpoint. As a species, we never developed any physical specializations. Almost everything we can do another species can do better. Other species can run faster, jump higher, climb better, track better, deal with heat better, survive cold better, swim better, see better, dig better, have sharper noses, have thicker hair and longer, sharper claws, reproduce faster... the list is endless, really.

The only things we can do better than any other species are (a) think; and (b) use tools (and other animals can do both to a lesser extent). Otherwise, everything we do, another species can do better. But very few species can do them *all* to some extent, the way we can. And as I pointed out earlier, those species are among our most annoying competitors—including rats, cockroaches, and weeds.

Not very flattering company, is it? But the point is, all these species are survivors. We adapt. We find ways to survive where nothing else can. Human beings have learned how to live everywhere on Earth, even in Antarctica, and we've even found ways to live in outer space. Unlike most species, we adapt through culture and invent things to help us survive, using our nimble fingers and big brains. Those represent two of the biological adaptations that we *do* have, and they're part of what makes it so easy for us to live anywhere, from the coldest, highest mountains, where the air is thin, to the hottest deserts, where it's almost too hot to breath.

Only the tougher species that, like humans, can learn to live on anything, anywhere, prosper in such environments. Gulls. Rats. Cockroaches. Coyotes. Rabbits. Weeds. Ironically, because they DO prosper and get in our way, we humans often call them pests—even when we have made them into what they are today—and we have whole industries dedicated to eradicating them wholesale, without even the dubious positive result of using them as food. If they had thumbs and big brains, we might be in big trouble!

One of our chief competitors for ruler of the world

A creature that can survive on any type of food, meat or vegetable, is called an *omnivore*. Biologically, human beings are omnivores. So are raccoons and bears. And because we're omnivores, if we know the basics of nutrition and know what's good for us, we can consciously decide not to eat meat. In other words, we can adopt an exploitation-free lifestyle BY CHOICE. Unlike wolves, we

35

don't have to eat only meat; just as unlike cows, we don't have to eat only vegeta-tion. But we *can* eat only vegetation if we want. We can also decide not to eat or use animal by-products, whether dairy foods or eggs or wool. We can decide to co-exist with the other creatures of this world in a natural balance that will en-sure that this world continues to exist, happy and healthy, indefinitely.

It really is as simple as that.

You don't have to eat meat. If you have cravings for meat, and your diet is properly balanced—not so hard to do—then those cravings are psychological. And one of the triumphs of humanity is that we can learn to ignore psychological urges to our benefit. Just as you can control your anger and live peacefully with everyone else, if you really want to, you can decide to become a Vegan and stick with your decision.

Notice I said that it was simple; but don't confuse that with easy. It won't be. An alcoholic or junkie almost never quits drugs or drinking overnight, and they often have to deal with physical withdrawal effects as well. Your withdrawal effects may or may not be physical once you decide to stop eating meat, but they will still be real, and really hard to overcome.

But you *can* overcome them, and in fact you should. It's in your best in-terests to stop eating meat, if only from a purely healthy perspective. From that point, of course, it's an easy jump to rejecting all animal products. As I've said before, we don't need them. Seriously.

Dietary Illnesses Caused by Meat-Eating

Did you know that there are certain illnesses directly caused by eating meat? One of them is gout. You don't hear much about this funny little disease anymore, because most people eat well-balanced diets with plenty of plant foods. Gout is caused by eating too much red meat. This causes a build-up of uric acid that causes arthritis, especially in the bones of the feet and toes, the deposit of little "chalkstones" (kind of like kidney stones), and acute pain. One of the main symptoms in the old days was searing pain in the big toe, of all places! The solution was simple: stop eating red meat.

Vegans don't get gout unless something else messes up their metabolism of uric acid, which can happen.

Heart disease. Obesity. Hypertension. Hardening of the arteries (arteriosclerosis). Contamination illnesses like trichinosis. All these and more can be caused or worsened by eating meat. According to the Academy of Nutrition and Dietetics, Vegans and vegetarians have a much lower risk of death caused by heart disease than the general population, and usually have lower blood pressure, are less likely to get Type 2 diabetes and cancer, and have lower cholesterol levels (especially if you let the sun convert it to Vitamin D!). We also tend to have lower BMIs, or Body Mass Indexes. While I won't say that there aren't fat Vegans, they aren't common.

This by itself is what saves us from high blood pressure and cancer. We just plain eat healthier than most people. Studies show that even people who eat healthy meats, like skinless chicken and fish high in Omega-3 and similar brain foods, tend to be less healthy than people who don't eat meat at all.

By not eating meat, we avoid contaminants that are common in modern meat, like *Salmonella, Campylobacter, E. coli, Listeria,* and other bacteria; artificial hormones; excess fat; and more. Vegans don't get trichinosis from poorly cooked pork, or other fluke and parasite disease. We don't contract mad cow disease, either. There are also a number of deficiency diseases that come from not eating enough vegetables. Scurvy, caused by a lack of Vitamin C, is probably the best known.

But recently, an acquaintance's sister suffered from a Vitamin K deficiency which made her ill and incoherent. It also impairs clotting—as it happens, she has known platelet issues—and bone development. My friend's sister had been going through a period in which she simply wasn't hungry, and was eating well below the recommended number of daily calories for a woman her age—including almost no leafy green vegetables. Turnip greens, spinach or kale would have helped her avoid this deficiency.

K is for Kale, an excellent source of Vitamin K

Overall, Vegans also tend to have stronger immune systems than meat-eaters. According to PETA, Vegans and vegetarians even live an average of 6-10 years longer than our friends and relatives who don't embrace the lifestyle. Most people would jump at the chance to extend their lives by 10% or more, and here's an easy way to do it!

A lot of people refuse to go Vegan or vegetarian because they say they don't want to lose the "flavor" that comes with eating meats and the attendant fats, and that they would miss the texture of meaty foods. But believe me, there's lots of flavor in plant foods. Even if you get bored, remember that almost all spices are made from plants. The only real exception is salt, which is the only rock that people can safely eat, and often do.

Almost all spices are plant products

Here's a startling fact: did you know that nearly all spices, including salt, were originally used *not* to add flavor to food, but to cover up the taste and smell of rot in meat products, or to keep rot from occurring in the first place? It's true. Pepper, paprika, cumin, and many other spices added a flavor that overpowered the taste of spoilage. Salt kept meat from spoiling by pulling out the moisture and killing bacteria. People just adapted (there's that word again) to the flavors of the spices they had to use, and came to prefer them; we all love Mom's home cooking, after all. People still adore their salt-cured hams. Smoking meats and otherwise drying them did the same thing. So did potting them with lots of their own fat; hence potted meat.

But back to the main show:

One thing that marketers know how to do well is present not just the benefits of a product or lifestyle, but also to list out and address objections to whatever they're selling. Now, everyone sells, not just marketers. Every time you try to bring someone over to your way of thinking, you're selling. So using that logic, I'm obviously selling the Vegan lifestyle I believe in.

I've already listed a lot of the healthy benefits of Veganism:

- **Longer life.**

- **Lower rates of obesity.**

- **Lower blood pressure.**

- **Lower cholesterol.**

- **Less cancer and diabetes.**

- **Significantly fewer food-borne diseases.**

- **Stronger immune systems.**

- **Overall good health.**

No, going Vegan won't keep you from being hit by a bus, and yes, sometimes even Vegans die suddenly from undiagnosed health problems. But those tragedies weren't caused by Vegan diets, the way some tragedies can be caused by carnivorous diets. All things being equal, Vegans tend to be healthier and live longer than non-Vegans. Hey, don't blame me, it's science.

So there are a bunch of easy-to-grasp benefits right there. Seriously, who doesn't want to live longer and feel better while doing it?

Come to the Vegan side. We have dark chocolate.

But people have all kinds of misconceptions about vegetarian and Vegan diets. I've already touched on some. People are always saying that "bunny food is bland." Come on, now. Think back to the last time you had a loaded baked potato, with salt, pepper, chives, with butter melting into it. Wasn't it savory and fulfilling? Replace the dairy butter with a butter made from coconut oil, cocoa butter, non-dairy milks, and lecithin, which is easy to find, and you have a purely Vegan meal. How about a baked sweet potato dusted with cinnamon? Vegan! Cinnamon toast, with or without margarine? Vegan! Dried banana chips? Vegan! That dark chocolate milk-free candy bar? Probably Vegan. (We avoid milk chocolate, of course.) Nuts, fruits, coconut, a lot of veggies—all flavorful, and fully Vegan.

There are so many tasty Vegan meals out there than the "bland" argument is baseless. Even things without strong flavors can be deeply satisfying to those who love them, spiced up or not. You can even make sour cream from a Vegan recipe. Jicama may not win any flavor awards, but its crisp starchiness can be refreshing. Want some great Vegan recipes to start on? Check the Appendix of this book.

Here's a big myth: *you need meat for protein.* No, you don't. Beans are full of protein. If you don't like some of the side effect of beans (which don't affect everyone), there are supplements to negate those effects. Other good sources of vegetable protein include:

- Amaranth

- Artichokes

- Asparagus

- Broccoli

- Chia seeds (yes, the same ones from Chia Pets!)

- Edamame (soy protein)

- Green peas

- Quinoa (pronounced "keen-wah")

- Lentils

- Nuts and nut butters of all kinds

- Soy milk

- Spinach

- Tempeh

- Tofu

Not enough protein in the Vegan diet? Nuts to that

Some worry that a Vegan diet lacks in oils and fats needed to maintain brain health, but a moment's thought will prove otherwise. Two rich oils produced from plants include peanut and olive oil; then there's canola oil, corn oil, and many more. You can cook in all kinds of oils, including special vegetable oils that contain fish-free Omega-3 fats necessary for good heart and brain function. Fish isn't the only brain food available; Brussels sprouts, winter squash, cauliflower, broccoli, and kale all contain decent amounts of Omega-3, with winter squash by far topping the list. This includes acorn, buttercup, butternut, pumpkins, spaghetti squashes, and more, all of which are really easy to grow. The softer summer squashes are better for carbohydrates than Omega-3, but they also make a tasty addition to your veggie mix—and again, they're easy to grow.

Winter squashes, including pumpkins, are full of Omega-3 fatty acids.

Some people argue that *Vegan diets are too full of carbs*, which can trigger or worsen Type II diabetes. This can actually be a problem, if you go into your diet without researching it first. But the same is true of a knee-jerk adoption of any diet, and even most of the scientists who argue for omnivorism as the best diet for humans admit that Vegans are more health-conscious than most people. We are careful to learn the nutritional content of what goes in our bellies, and are more likely to balance our carbs than other people. Health is largely a matter of awareness, especially dietary awareness.

Lacto-vegetarians sometimes retain dairy in their diets mostly because they worry about their bones; this is especially true for women, who, due to our metabolisms, lose more calcium and iron than men do. This is also an argument non- Vegans use against the lifestyle. However, there are plenty of calcium sources for us that don't come from milk, cheese, and the like. Bok choy (a.k.a. pak choi, or Chinese cabbage), broccoli, collard greens, kale, mustard greens, okra, soy milk, and calcium-set tofu all have lots of calcium. If you still can't get enough or don't like those foods, then you can take calcium pills or drink special calcium drinks. Just make sure the drinks and pills don't contain animal products. Some calcium is made from oyster shells, which some Vegans may consider acceptable if they are old and long since discarded by the oysters that made them; but they're still animal products. Calcium made in the lab or ground from rocks may be better, though calcium not already in plants can be really hard for the body to digest and absorb.

And no, you don't have to eat bloody meat to get iron for your diet, either—which is, again, especially important to the ladies. Most legumes (lentils, beans, and peanuts) have enough for your needs, as do fortified cereals, quinoa, brown rice, oatmeal, and many nuts, as well as spinach, chard, and mustard greens. Wow, these food lists are making me drool! Luckily, many of these foods are easily cooked in a variety of ways, from salads to sautéed and spiced veggies. You can even use some of the greens in sandwiches instead of lettuce.

Think you'll miss sweets if you go Vegan? As if! We've got most of the sugars, just as long as it's not white sugar—which is dried with bone char from animals (another thing most people don't realize). While we don't do honey, since it's a product of bees and that would be a form of animal exploitation, even honey comes from flower nectar. Otherwise, we've got fruits, berries, stevia, agave nectar, and sugar beets—which also provide edible greens!

Please excuse me while my stomach growls.

I think you get the point. All it takes to maintain a healthy Vegan diet is a careful eye on what you eat. If you want to avoid deficiency diseases, there are easily obtained foods you can add to your diet all the way around. Even if some of them like lentils, chia, and quinoa sound a little exotic, you can find them in your local Whole Foods Market or Grocery Store. Even if you can't, there's this little thing called the Internet that lets you order food from all over the world that can be sent straight to your door in days. You can get the best polenta, jarred peppers, and plenty of other good stuff for decent prices, and you don't have to wait forever for it to arrive, either, if you join Amazon Prime! Hey, it's only $100 a year as I write this. That's worth it to make the world a better place!

Sweet, delicious berries

If nothing else, Vegan diets are healthier than omnivorous ones because we also avoid things like refined sugar, over-processed foods, trans-fats, and other additives and chemicals (even natural ones) that are just plain bad for us. It's an easy way to stay healthy and keep the world safe for the 99.99999999+% of species that aren't human beings, but still have a valid claim to the planet.

Speaking of which, brace yourself. We're about to enter painful territory, the part of this discussion that I feel is the most convincing of the arguments against killing animals for food or otherwise exploiting them for their body products.

Next comes the chapter where I discuss ethical arguments for Veganism. Be sure to keep any eye out for the caution symbol if you want to avoid the worse discussions... and be prepared to see it a lot.

My apologies in advance. The livestock, fisheries, and fur preparation industries are brutal—and a detailed discussion of them is necessary to make my point. You can rest assured I'll be washing my mind out with soap afterward.

Chapter 3: Ethical Arguments for Veganism

If Steven Spielberg's ET ever really came to visit, I suspect the gentle botanist would conclude that despite our relatively advanced civilization, humanity is broken—and one of his chief arguments would be our meat-producing industry. Yes, humanity is also broken because we sometimes dehumanize others, and commit mass genocide. However, I would argue that despite the evidence of Nazi Germany, Yugoslavia, and Rwanda in the past century, this is becoming less common. As horrible as it is, it doesn't occur constantly.

But every year, we deliberately kill tens of billions of animals, just to feed our hunger... and because, in most religions, the people who interpret the word of God tells us this is okay.

Yet I would argue that killing in any form desensitizes us to suffering. It teaches each new generation that raising droves of animals in horrific, demeaning environments and then killing them for their flesh, fur, feathers, skin, organs, brains, claws, beaks, and other body parts is acceptable. We all know it happens, but most of us hide our eyes and accept its results anyway, because we have convinced ourselves that we need those products. Even animals that are not killed, just exploited for their hair, fluids, or reproductive materials, are treated poorly in almost every case.

Our justification is that we don't have to dehumanize animals, you see—because they're not human already. We're taught they don't have souls, or can't really feel pain as we know it, or are just unthinking bundles of instinctive reactions, good for little more than service to the reasoning, refined beings we perceive ourselves to be. We view all animals as lesser beings, a lesson emphasized not just in church but in school and most sciences.

Look: Animals have an overwhelming desire to live programmed into their very genes, which means that they're nearly always dragged down into death screaming and unwillingly. This is doubly awful, because in a modern age where we know how to make food and everything else we need from non-animal sources, killing and/or exploiting animals is by no means necessary!

So why do we do it? Because we are thoughtless, tradition-bound, and perhaps not nearly as ethically advanced as we like to think. I would add lazy, but the fact is, it takes serious effort to kill an animal that doesn't want to die, even if that just involves designing the right machinery to do it. It's probably easier to grow and harvest plants, all things considered.

African elephants, once killed mostly for their overgrown teeth

It's nice that we've made it illegal to collect most ivory, for example, but we still use what we have—mostly for artistic reasons, as we have from tens of thousands of years, when the sources were mammoths and mastodons instead of elephants and walruses. Many see nothing wrong with using old ivory, since it already exists. But that argument can be used for all kinds of materials that "already exist," including some truly reprehensible stuff, like the research collected by Nazi physicians who conducted horrible experiments on the people they suppressed and slaughtered. You can argue that you didn't do it yourself, and yes, its origins are reprehensible; but since it already exists, you might as well take advantage of it. But if we were to reject such things altogether, as both depraved and beneath us, that might have a greater effect on our cultural and ethical evolution.

For those who argue that some of the meat dishes we eat and the products we collect from animals are necessary to maintain tradition, I would say: ***Old traditions can be broken, and new ones established.*** In my home state of Texas, a century-old tradition at Texas A&M University was abandoned after 1999 when the student-built bonfire under construction collapsed, killing 12 and injuring 37. Three years later, Aggie Bonfire was resurrected as a privately funded, well-organized non-profit off-campus activity with strict safety rules and building guides, something that had not existed before.

My point is that one of the strengths of humanity is that we can adapt to all kinds of new things—and change our minds about old ones. If we couldn't, old traditions would still have us living in trees, eating bugs. Primitive hominids may not have had to work hard (less than 20 hours a week to survive, some experts think), but the eating bugs part most of us can live without... along with getting rained on constantly, surviving the cold with neither fire nor clothing, picking lice out of our hair, and dying of old age at 30.

One argument I've heard against Veganism and vegetarianism is that not all arable land can be used for human food production. A lot of it is rocky, gets flooded too often, doesn't have the right kind of soil, is located on sleep stopes, etc. That's one argument agriculturalists use to justify raising livestock: they can use the land we can't, and can convert plant foods we can't into protein-rich, fat-rich meat. That's true—but! We also use a lot of our arable land to grow animal feed like grain and hay. If we didn't eat animals, we could *still* free up millions of hectares now used only for that purpose. We could grow corn for people, not cows. We might even figure out ways to turn that non-edible plant food into something we could use, like bio-gas and other organic fuels. Sawgrass, for example, yields useful biodiesel when processed.

Even some of the food we consider "animal food grade," like low-quality corn, is edible by humans, and often doesn't taste so bad. Sometimes, only prejudice keeps us from eating it. For example: black-eyed peas, a.k.a. cowpeas. They're called cowpeas for a reason, because they used to be fed only to cows.

***The black-eyed peas in this bean salad were once believed
to be fit only for animal food***

But during the Civil War, when whole armies foraged through farming areas and took everything they considered edible, they often left only the cowpeas and similar stuff—because they were grown as animal food. The impoverished people left behind, especially poor blacks and slaves, only had cowpeas left to eat.

Well, they discovered what most of us Vegans have: that when properly cooked, black-eyed peas have a rich, earthy flavor that goes well with cabbage and corn-bread. Now black-eyed peas are a staple of southern cuisine and soul food, much like red beans and rice—the traditional easy-to-cook meal for Monday laundry days in Louisiana. Black-eyed peas and cabbage, known as "Hoppin' John," is now a traditional New Year's Day food for Southern whites and blacks all over the country, because it's considered good luck.

The Sickening

I've already discussed the sheer numbers of animals we kill just for food. The death toll stands at at least 56 billion animals *per year*. That's about eight animals per person per year on this planet—and you know that people in developed countries get a much larger amount of meat per capita per year than everyone else. And this only includes land animals deliberately raised for slaughter! Who knows how many more hunted animals, fish, shellfish, and other sea creatures should be added to the toll?

At this rate of consumption, if we had been around in the days of the dinosaurs, we would probably have wiped them from the face of the planet. There's evidence that we did at least contribute to the extinction of at least some of the last of the giant Ice Age animals called *megafauna*—mammoths, mastodons, giant sloths, saber-toothed tigers, most North American camels, North American horses, giant bison and more—in most parts of the world starting about 20,000 years or so ago, as human big-game hunters really got their act together. We can safely say we didn't know better then. We do now.

At least most countries aren't still hunting whales, thank goodness. But we love our fish; indeed, an innovative and celebrated chef was blamed for practically wiping out the redfish population in the Gulf of Mexico due to the popularity of his signature dish in the 1980s and 1990s. Fortunately, conservation efforts are bringing back the redfish population today. As I've mentioned before, this has happened repeatedly with other species of fish, especially those captured by "factory ships" that use incredibly huge nets to siphon in everything and process it on the spot in a dangerous 24-hour environment. These ships use every trick they can, from blowers on the bottom of conveyor belts to deliberately miscalibrated scales, to illegally over harvest their quota of fish—which, needless to say, is already too large to be sustainable. And anyone who's ever watched *The Deadliest Catch* knows that those fisherman cram as many crabs into their holds as they can, often literally stomping them down, even at risk of the crabs at the bottom dying before they return to the shore and offload... even though, like dead lobsters and crawfish, dead crabs are rejected as just so much wasted organic matter.

With the popularity of these varieties of seafood, along with shrimp and oysters, and the dependence of many nations on sea creatures for a large percentage of their food, the real numbers of annual animal deaths are probably in the trillions. It amazes me that Mother Earth can absorb so many deaths per year and still keep functioning. But then again, maybe she can't for much longer, as I'll discuss in the next chapter. Admittedly, a large percentage of those deaths are from rather small animals like fish, shellfish, and krill... but a death is a death, and it diminishes us all.

Despite the efforts of people like Temple Grandin, the conditions in the livestock industry in particular remain shockingly inhumane. The industry treats animals as things, not as living beings—just commodities on the hoof. This may partly be in an effort to distance themselves from what they believe they have to do; maybe some of the people in the industry are just numb to the reality after facing and causing so much death. Some of the people in the industry, though, either don't care, are deliberately cruel, or just too stupid to know what they're doing. Too often, the animals in question are mistreated and miserably overcrowded their whole lives, from the time they're born until their untimely deaths.

Smart agriculturalists treat their animals better, mostly by allowing them to free-range during their lifetimes, finding their own food but supplementing it with daily feedings of high-protein and mineral-rich foods—often partly made from rotten oranges, leftover vegetables, the remains of their own kind, and whatever else can be inexpensively added. These ranchers also give their animals hormones, plenty of medicines to make sure they don't get sick, and otherwise do what they can to keep them happy right up until they're herded into a truck and taken to a slaughterhouse.

The animals aren't well-treated because the people raising them are kind or progressive. The *only* reason these animals are treated better is to ensure they're healthy and produce fewer "culls" that can't be used for making into dinners for humans. But in the end, even well-treated animals are stuffed full of antibiotics that increase bacterial resistance year after year, an unfortunate side effect of wholesale modern meat production, as well as steroids and other hormones intended to increase the amount of meat per animal and, ideally, to make it "taste better." But does it really?

And are these medications completely metabolized, or do they build up in the tissues of these animals, as some scientists think they might? If that's true, consider what all those medications might be doing to those who eat the animals that were pumped full of them. Is it any wonder that many people have begun to demand hormone-free meat?

A healthy, happy hog, unaware of its fate

Better that they demand no meat at all, even if only because *claiming* meat is clean of steroids and antibiotics doesn't mean it's so. Ideally, I would hope they would eschew meat instead because they've matured ethically. If a person can't shake the psychological need to eat meat—remember, there is no *physical* need for it—then they can always eat textured vegetable protein that looks, smells, and tastes like meat, but is made from soybeans. Some people can't even tell the difference.

Slaughterhouse Five Billion

I really, really hope that you've never had the occasion to smell a slaughterhouse, and never do. There are few smells more putrid and vomit-inducing. Even those addicted to meat will admit that. I live in Texas, where we have a lot of chemical plants and paper mills along the Gulf Coast. I've smelled them sometimes passing through Houston or Corpus Christi, and boy do they smell bad. But slaughterhouses smell ten times worse—at least. Compared to them, a sewage plant smells like a rose garden.

I assure you, I am NOT exaggerating.

Imagine a place where cattle, pigs, and other large animals are packed into holding pens in their thousands—places where they are constantly fearful, and aware that their fellow animals keep disappearing and not coming back. The smell of distress permeates the area. It's joined by the voiding of bladders and bowels in the normal course of events, multiplying the barnyard smell tenfold.

Worse, the animals—and you—can smell the all-pervading scent of old, rotten blood, which sears the nostrils and claws the throat. It never goes away. Even humans can smell it for miles when the wind is right. Most animals have more sensitive noses than we do, and naturally avoid the smell of blood because it's frightening. It means death is near, and normally they would turn tail and run. When they're packed into the cattle pens, though, they can't escape it. They can't get away. They can barely move, increasing their fear and sense of impending doom.

Animals may be speechless, but they can feel emotions, especially the large, complex animals we use for food. Pigs are considered the most intelligent animals in the barnyard. Even cows are not as stupid as we commonly think. They can tell when something horrible is coming. It's hard to imagine how these animals feel as they wait to die. We have human parallels from concentrations and death camps, though. Maybe, like the people who knew they were going to die short of a miracle, the animals just give up, and wait in a sort of numb stupor for the end to come. Maybe their minds just switch off. Maybe they go quietly insane. This might be for the best, because the overcrowded conditions are just a prelude for what is to come.

A historic stockyard. Note the crowding in the nearest pen

Sometimes—and this is rare—they do try to escape, only to be stopped and beaten down, or killed in place.

The worst thing about all this may be just how casually the slaughterhouses treat the process. In many cases—despite the efficiency efforts of Temple Grandin and others—slaughterhouses are poorly designed. Most aren't as bad as they used to be, but they're still bad. Little thought and less care is given for the animals' comfort or safety; why bother, since they'll be dead in hours? The floors are either constantly muddy, plain dirt poisoned with animal waste, or made of scarred wooden boards or slippery metal grates that provide poor footing when thousands of scared animals are eliminating on them daily. The cattle are forced to move in straight, regimented lines, one-by-one, which is not natural for a herd animal. Broken legs and necks aren't uncommon when animals slip, as they're hurried along to their deaths.

An empty slaughterhouse. Note the plywood and dirt floors.

In the name of efficiency, the livestock are usually herded down a maze of chutes, one at a time and none-too-gently. Sometimes they're hurried along by people with pointed rods or electrified cattle-prods. If an animal falls, it's likely to break one of its long, relatively spindly legs. Too bad. It's either killed immediately and pulled out of the way, or forced to move on anyway. When it finally gets inside and to the head of the line, it's met by its killer. Its head is usually locked in place with a kind of metal collar before the end comes. In the old days—a few decades ago—a strong man called a "knocker" swung a sledgehammer into the animal's forehead to kill it, striking a specific vulnerable spot right in the center. A good knocker could put the animal down immediately. Others weren't so efficient.

A modern captive bolt gun used for killing livestock in a slaughterhouse

More common now is the "humane" captive bolt-gun, which can be used at very high speed. Most are built with a sliding bolt affixed in the barrel on a piston. Either pneumatic air pressure or a special blank, a cartridge without a bullet but otherwise complete, drives the bolt an inch or so out of the barrel into whatever the barrel is pressed against. Instead of having to swing a big hammer at the vulnerable spot, the killer just puts the barrel up to that spot and pulls the trigger.

The bolt penetrates the animal's skull and continues into the brain, at the least rendering it unconscious and usually killing it instantly. The animal goes down immediately. It's better than a sledgehammer to the head, but it's still awful.

After the animal is safely dead, it's hooked to a chain and lifted with a crane to the location where it will be reduced to meat and various by-products like leather, hair, dog chews, bone meal, blood meal, catfish blood bait, and a hundred other things.

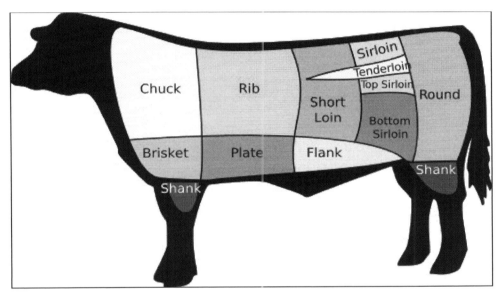

No part of the cow is wasted

The above process is the one most often used for cattle, pigs, goats, sheep, and other large mammals. It may differ in detail from slaughterhouse to slaughterhouse, but that's more or less how it goes. By the way, as of 2015 in the United States, there were only about 148 slaughter inspectors total. That's about one per million animals slaughtered in the U.S. each year.

One more cruelty these creatures have to suffer: they're marked to identify them from birth to death. In the old days, hot iron templates were used to brand an identifying pattern on the animal's flank, creating a painful scar. Now they're more likely to have a plastic tag attached to an ear. This is much more painful than our practice of ear-piercing for fashion purposes; the hole required may be the diameter of a pencil. Sometimes, it gets infected and the animal suffers; other times, the tag may get torn off on a bush or a tree, scarring the animal for life. But no worries: the rancher just pumps it full of more antibiotics.

Typical slaughterhouse output

The Fate of Poultry

Poultry are often slaughtered in a different and more efficient way than mammals. This does not, however, mean it is more respectful to the animal or in any way humane; in fact, it's even less so. Often, chickens, turkeys, ducks, and the like are hung up on chains and pulled along a conveyor past spinning horizontal blades, something like buzz saws, that cut their throats or just plain cut off their heads. They then proceed to bleed out as they are moved along to the place where their feathers are stripped off and their bodies are reduced to meat, often by completely mechanical means. If you've ever seen a product like potted meat or Vienna sausage that claims to be made of "mechanically separated" chicken, turkey, etc., this is how it's done.

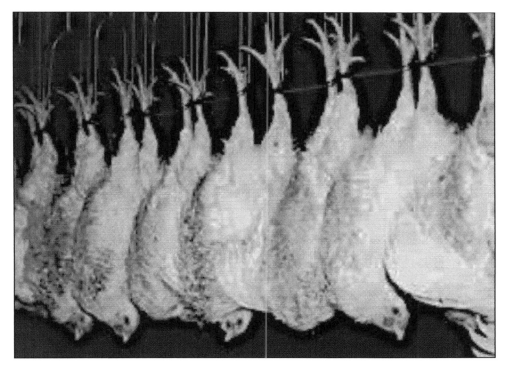

No, I wasn't exaggerating. These chickens are alive and aware

It's not just a horrible way to die, it has to be terrifying as they're jerked along the conveyer, slowly approaching the blades and seeing those ahead of them die, one after the other. This is the fate of many male chickens, females not selected to be egg layers ("pullets"), and layers who have been exhausted of their reproductive capabilities after spending their lives in tiny cages, doing nothing but eating, creating fertilizer (poop), and pumping out eggs.

The Horror of Veal

Even some meat eaters refuse to eat veal, simply because of the completely degrading and inhumane way it's produced. There can be no free-range veal, because that would ruin the intent. The idea here is to produce the most tender beef possible, and there's only one way to do that: "harvest" it from young calves that have never used their muscles and have fed only on protein-rich milk.

There's only one way to make sure a calf doesn't use its muscles: *never let it move.* One way is to harvest the calves as they are born. In days past, this was the fate of many male calves born to dairy cows, which are kept constantly pregnant to make sure they continue to produce milk. This is still done sometimes; the calves are killed at just a few days old to produce a low-grade veal called "bob veal" that's often used in cheap TV dinners. So if you've ever eaten a beef TV dinner, you may have eaten veal without even knowing it.

Today, male calves are more commonly emasculated and raised as steers for meat. It's more efficient to raise veal another way—by letting them grow up for a few months before slaughter. Most veal calves are shoved into tight slatted crates six feet long and two feet wide with chains around their necks, where they

Seriously, do you really want one of these little guys in your TV dinner?

can only lie down or stand. They can't turn around, stretch, or otherwise move much, other than to toss their heads, chew the air, scratch, and kick—stress behavior for cattle. They literally cannot move around any farther than that for the entirety of their short lives; after all, the ranchers don't want their muscles to develop. Their mostly-liquid diet is deliberately deficient in iron and fiber, so they become anemic. This is so their meat will take on the pale hue and tender nature that makes it such a delicacy. They are allowed no bedding, not even straw, for fear that they will eat it and it will provide the iron and fiber they crave, ruining the quality of their meat. Veal calves are forced to lie in their own waste... if they're allowed to lie down. Like factory farmed chickens, all they can do is eat and make fertilizer, which you can bet that the ranchers make the most of. Livestock ranchers and their slaughterhouses are nothing if not efficient, which helps them lower the cost of meat, making it easier for anyone to buy—and easier to cheapen the lives of the animals they raise. By the time they're deemed old enough to slaughter, at an age of 16-20 weeks—about the equivalent age of four-year-old children—veal calves can't even walk. They are then killed, bled out, and processed with special care, so as not to damage the pale, tender meat that gourmands and chefs love, because it practically "melts in the mouth."

A veal calf, approaching slaughtering age, locked in its cramped crate

You can no doubt guess how lamb chops are produced, just so people can enjoy them with their mint jelly. The process is similar to veal, though more often the lambs are simply taken from their mothers when they're large enough to be worth harvesting.

A similar process results in the Hispanic dish known as "cabrito," which translates to "little goat." Need I spell out where that particular tender meat, which is often barbecued in festivals like the one held in Brady, Texas every year, comes from?

In all these cases, animals are slaughtered before they've had a chance to live. Better for them never to have been born at all than to be snuffed out so soon.

Cabrito on the hoof

Dairy Origins

Dairy cows have it better than veal, but not by much. Most dairy cows come from specialized breeds like Guernseys, Holsteins, and Jerseys that have been bred and overbred for hundreds of years to do little more than produce milk. As I've already mentioned, they are kept constantly pregnant, since the milk is intended by nature for their babies, and overbred to produce huge amounts of milk—as much as a gallon or more at a time. Can you imagine that much fluid in one udder? Most are allowed to wander free and feed on grass, since that's considered the best feedstock for milk production, but many are also fed hay, vitamins, and nutrients to enrich their milk and encourage further milk production. That's on top of all the hormones and antibiotics they're dosed with on a regular basis. It gets to the point for most cows that if they aren't promptly milked once or twice a day, their udders get painfully full. If they aren't milked on time, their udders may rupture, causing severe injury and even death.

Nope, too inefficient for modern agriculture

The milking process is not exactly a paragon of gentleness. Forget the idea of people milking by hand. That takes too long. Cows have a number of teats that dangle from their udders that, normally, their babies would suckle to get the milk. Modern dairy farmers attach hoses to each teat that lead to a mechanical milking machine. The milk is drawn out as fast as possible and added to the milk from a hundred other cows, mixed together, and pumped into a liquids hauler truck. It's then taken to the factory to be filtered and processed.

Afterward, the cow is allowed to go about its business. If she's lucky, she lives on a farm where she's allowed to feed on grass until her udder gets full again, whereupon she voluntarily returns to the barn for more milking. It's that or be in constant pain. If she's unlucky, she lives in a little stall she rarely leaves, amid her own wastes.

A rotary milking parlor in Australia, courtesy of Wikipedia's Cgoodwin

Needless to say, dairy cow calves are usually taken away from them as soon as they're born, to meet a fate as veal, steers, or future dairy cows themselves, if they're healthy and female. And what happens when a dairy cow is too old to produce more babies and, therefore, more milk? Most are not put out to pasture to live out the rest of their lives peacefully. That would not be cost efficient. They're sent to the slaughterhouse, sometimes just to be made into dog food because they're too old and tough for steaks.

Wool Producers

You might think that animals raised only for the harvests of their hair, like sheep, some goats, alpacas, and llamas, have it easy—because most of them don't wind up eaten. Not true. Their lives might be easy compared to a cow's, assuming their owners are progressive and moderately sensible, but it's still a life of slavery and exploitation that often ends in an ignoble death.

These animals, like dairy cows, have been overbred for a single, specific purpose: to produce clothing fibers. While these fibers are 100% organic, soft, and wonderfully warm, they can easily be replaced by fleece made from, of all things, plastic bottles—as well as other artificial materials that clever people are constantly coming up with. Some of these animals have been so overbred (which is sometimes done by breeding them with close relatives, including mothers, fathers, and siblings), that otherwise rare genetic defects become common. One example is the famous fainting goat breed, which when startled literally freeze up and fall over. People play this for laughs, deliberately scaring the animals over and over to see their reactions, but it's not funny. It's a form of animal cruelty.

When fiber-producing animals are sheared, they're often treated roughly because the shearers don't care about them one bit except as sources of hair. If fact, the shearers sometimes pride themselves on how quickly they can shear an animal—some can shear a sheep in less than a minute. Not surprisingly, accidental injuries, from broken bones to lacerations from the shears, are not uncommon. Of course, the sheep ranchers know that they'll make more money from an animal that lives longer, but this doesn't keep inexpert handling by workers moving too fast from hurting the animal, especially if the animal struggles.

I don't have to tell you what happens to animals who are born with obvious defects, who get too old, or simply become superfluous. They're sent to the slaughterhouse to be made into pet food; after all, mutton and goat aren't as popular as beef or pork, and people tend not to eat llamas and their relatives in the U.S. Some of them don't even get that far. If the rancher doesn't want to be bothered, he'll kill the animals and toss them into the woods, as an archaeologist acquaintance of mine discovered while looking for sites near a mohair goat farm.

He discovered a goat "graveyard" near a stream, where dead animals had created a huge mass of exposed bone. Because the heads and hides were missing, it took a zoologist specializing in bone identification to determine what the remains were, because the archaeologist didn't recognize them as he would have those of wild animals or cattle.

Adult sheep ready to be shorn, with lamb chops on the side

Draft, Riding, and Racing Animals

One of the original purposes for domesticating large animals was for them to serve as draft animals and to bear humans on their backs to speed up our ability to get from here to there faster. It was a way to increase our muscle power with natural machines that "burned" hay or grass. In fact, even today, this concept is so engrained in our culture that we still use the term "horsepower" to rate the power of many automotive and other motors.

The original horsepower. Note the brands

Although this practice is no longer necessary, it's still practiced in some parts of the world where people could be using motors to pull wagons or to conduct farming. It's even still done in the United States, by religious groups who don't believe in using many, if any, machines to do work. While I can respect other people's cultural beliefs, too often they are used as excuses to continue mistreating animals. Just as some cultural groups are still allowed to sacrifice animals for religious reason and to harvest endangered animals like whales and salmon—yes, even in North America—because it's traditional, others still ride in horse-drawn buggies, use plows drawn by oxen, horse, mules, and donkeys to prepare fields for planting, and use the same animals for harvesting. Why? Because they can. But there's no need for it, as most of the developed world has realized. Motorized machines can do the work faster and more efficiently. Although they're often more expensive than draft animals, they can pay for themselves more quickly, and often last longer. Many's the 1950s John Deere tractor still in service.

Serving as draft beasts wears animals out before their time. While some owners may be careful with their investments, many are not, and are less willing to allow them to heal when injured than car or tractor owners are to repair their vehicles when they break down. Draft animals are often shot dead when they become lame, since their long legs are very difficult to treat. Unsentimental owners are likely to sell older animals to slaughterhouses or knackers when they can no longer perform, for conversion into meat, soap, and glue. Until a few years ago, there were still horse slaughterhouses in my home state of Texas where agents brought in horses to be slaughtered for their meat to be sold in Europe. They got horses from farms wanting to dispose of old mares who couldn't have any more babies and geldings who could no longer work, as well as from riders who just got tired of taking care of their horses. Old riding and racing horses who get too old or become injured were disposed the same way.

Until recently, racing dogs like greyhounds and hunting dogs like beagles were often killed or abandoned when they had outlived their usefulness, were not genetically "pure," or had congenital problems (due to rampant inbreeding) that kept them from racing or tracking. These practices are much less common now, with the rise of breed-specific rescue societies.

A pet greyhound—and fellow Texan judging from the shape of its tag!

Incidentally: like cows used to be, most horses are often still painfully branded using ultra-hot or ultra-cold irons. Racehorses are more likely to be tattooed on the insides of their lips with a registry number.

Fur bearing Agony

As awful as livestock ranching can be, especially when the animals are sent to the slaughterhouse, I'm sorry to say that it pales in comparison to how fur bearing animals like beaver, chinchillas, ermines, foxes, mink, muskrat, nutria, opossums, rabbits, and raccoons are treated. These animals are either raised specifically for their furs, whereupon they are usually killed before they reach adulthood, or "harvested" from the wild using cruel traps. Typically, the meat is wasted, dumped to rot regardless of the health hazards, even though many of these animals are edible.

If you're surprised that some of those animals are used for fur coats, it's because it's a closely guarded secret. Nutria, also called coypu or water rats, are a South American species that has invaded the Southern states in the last hundred years. Think of them as giant muskrats. They are also similar to beavers except their tails are round in cross-section, like a muskrat's, and their fur isn't as soft. But their fur can be shorn of the coarse outer hairs and passed off as beaver or muskrat, important furs for coats in colder parts of the world where fur is still commonly worn, like Eastern Europe and the former Soviet Union. Opossums, on the other hand, have marvelously soft, gray fur that is sometimes dyed and passed off as rabbit fur. Rabbit fur coats (a profitable by-product of the rabbit

The humble nutria

meat industry in countries all over the world) were popular in the U.S. during the 1980s, but have long since gone out of style. Even hamsters are raised for their pelts in some fur farms, believe it or not! In prehistoric times, they were also hunted for food in Eurasia.

The truth is, the fur industry would use rats as fur bearers if they were big enough, their fur soft enough, and their coats could be passed off as something else—if they could get away with it. I have this on good authority from someone who once worked in the industry. And in China, I was shocked to learn, dogs and cats are raised in fur farms and slaughtered by the millions, their furs passed off as something else. PETA has discovered that many of the animals in dog and cat fur farms *still wear collars*, indicating they were stolen from owners left to wonder what happened to their beloved companion animals. Cruella De Vil's Dalmatian fur coat doesn't seem so far-fetched now, does it?

The scary looking opossum, which has the softest fur ever

Traditionally, most furs were gathered by independent trappers who then sold them to fur-buyers. Don't assume that this is a dead practice. While it doesn't pay nearly as well now that fur is being farmed and has become much less popular, to this very day it's possible to obtain a trapper's license and set out traps on public land, or on private land with permission.

Old-fashioned leg-hold traps are still used by trappers of wild animals. All of the above animals I've already listed, along with coyotes, bobcats, lynxes, and even skunks, are deliberately caught in this way, using various types of sets. The traps snap shut so strongly the animals can't escape unless they're willing to gnaw off a leg. Some do. Some who do that survive, but many die soon after from blood-loss or infection, or simply can't continue to compete for food in the wild and starve to death.

Those who don't are left to the mercy of the trapper, who kills the animal before taking it out of the trap. Because a bullet hole would damage the fur, the trapper usually clubs the animal to death with a long billet of hardwood, striking them on the back of the head until they die. This is a particularly difficult process with opossums, which are very hard to kill and are willing to play dead until they can escape—so they sometimes undergo this cruel, painful process repeatedly.

More recently, instant kill traps have come into use. These are rectangular traps, generically known as "conibears" after a popular manufacturer, that attract the animal to stick its head in them to get the bait. When the trap springs, it crushes the animal's skull or breaks its neck. The problem with these traps is that if a free-ranging pet triggers one, they don't get a second chance to survive as they might in a leg-hold trap. They're dead on the spot, again leaving grieving owners to wonder what happened to their missing pets. Conibears and leg-hold traps alike also leave litters of baby animals to starve to death if the mother is trapped.

An orphaned baby raccoon

Because trapping is difficult and requires so much killing, independent trappers have begun to die out as fur prices have plummeted over the past 40 years. There was a time as recently as the early 1980s when a good raccoon pelt could bring $25 or more, with a bobcat, coyote, mink, or fox bringing much more. Those days are gone as fur prices have dropped precipitously in the U.S. and other industrialized nations. These days, even large raccoon furs from colder areas rarely bring more than $3 each. Now trappers are more likely to earn their money ridding areas of "nuisance" animals whose populations have increased as fur prices have decreased.

Today, most furs come from fur farms, where animals are raised only to be killed for their furs. It takes a special kind of cruelty—or appalling ability to turn your mind off—to own or work on a fur farm. I'm going to go into this only briefly due to its gruesomeness.

A mink, the most commonly farmed fur bearer

Animals raised only for their fur are typically fed on meat by-products not considered fit for human consumption. Sometimes they're fed on the corpses of animals previously killed on the fur farm. Often, they receive supplements and vitamins to increase the quality of the fur in their pelts. They're usually kept in small, filthy cages where they can take only a few steps at a time and that they never leave for the rest of their lives, except when they are bred to other animals or, in the case of females, when they bear their litters. Not all females are used for reproduction, as nursing their babies enlarges their teats, which makes their pelts unattractive. These females are basically used for baby factories, in the same sense that these farms are fur factories. Stress, fear, pain, parasitic infections, exhaustion, and illness are constant companions.

When a fur bearing animal is deemed large enough to produce a decent-sized pelt without getting so large as to produce a coarse one, it is killed. For minks, the most commonly farmed fur bearing animal (followed by foxes), this occurs when they are six months old. Of course, they are killed in a way that won't damage the pelt. One of the most common ways is to jam electrodes into the animal's anus and mouth and turn on a high current, painfully electrocuting the animal and causing death by heart attack while still conscious. Others are clubbed to death, have their necks broken, are slowly bled to death from small wounds made in areas not covered by fur, suffocated via strychnine poisoning, and poisoned using vehicle exhaust.

The vehicle exhaust method doesn't work very well, and sometimes animals wake up as they're being skinned.

Enough said.

Killing Our Souls

Killing animals on a massive scale when we don't have to do so is killing our souls. It was bad enough when people knew of no other way to survive, were limited in what they could eat, or were ignorant of the fact that they could live nutritionally healthy lives without eating meat. Now that we know better it's a travesty. Ignoring it won't save us psychologically. It will only make our society more callous and awful. Even exploiting animals for renewable resources like milk, eggs, and hair is a kind of slavery. Some may argue that these animals exist only for this reason, that they're doing what they're designed for—but we designed them that way, not God. Only through thousands of years of domestication have they become the "cash cows" (sometimes literally) that we know today. We have taken certain animals who have certain attributes we like and monetized them to be raised and exploited in factories where they are treated callously at best. If we had left them alone, they would be living out their lives in the wild, subject to the whims of nature—not humanity. Yes, there might be fewer of many species, especially the large mammals now raised as livestock and used as draft animals—cows, horses, mules, donkeys, pigs, goats, sheep, llamas, alpacas, oxen, and the like—but only because the land's carrying capacity would limit their populations. Nature may be cruel, but it's not a deliberate cruelty.

As I have already pointed out, all this killing, maiming, and exploitation undermines our ethical evolution. Our ethics have trended upward for centuries, despite the fact that mass genocide still occurs, led by insane but charismatic leaders. We're left aghast to wonder how such things could happen—in Germany, in Bosnia, in Rwanda, in the Caucasus, in Darfur. Meanwhile we don't even think about the tens of billions of large animals we kill each year for food, the countless numbers of creatures we drag from the sea to suffocate or boil alive for the same reason, the many millions who die for fur coats, hats, and stoles, and the billions more that we exploit for the products of their bodies—from hooves for gelatin to feathers for pillows, from half-and-half for our coffee to wool for our sweaters, from leather for couches and sports cars to pharmaceutical products to treat human illnesses.

We even mutilate our pets for reasons of tradition and style. Pit bulls and Dobermans aren't born with pointed ears and stumpy tails. Although some dog breeds do have naturally erect, pointy ears, especially those most closely related to wolves—the various shepherds, huskies, malamutes, and the like—one of the most distinct differences between dogs and wolves is that only dogs have floppy ears. And even dog breeds famous for lacking tails, like the schipperke, are *born* with tails. They're just "docked" after they're born.

Forget about video games and television desensitizing us to violence. There's a much bigger culprit that we tend to ignore. Most of us, even those who have never been on a farm or worked in the industry, know that all this horrific killing happens every single day, *but we deliberately don't think about it.* Isn't this the same kind of thinking that leads to horrors like female genital mutilation and racial persecution? Could this be why serial killers usually start out by mistreating and killing animals before they graduate to humans?

It's something worth thinking about. And you have to wonder: what are we going to come to if this goes on? What would the people of another planet think if they discovered us and realized the endless suffering and death we promote?

Maybe that's why we haven't met any yet. Maybe they think we're barbarians.

Or maybe they're just scared of us.

Chapter 4: Ecological Arguments for Veganism

We live in a disposable society. In the modern era, we would rather just throw something away and buy a new one than try to save or conserve it, no matter what the resource. This attitude applies to everything from aluminum cans to automobiles, and I feel it extends to animals as well. It may be one reason almost everyone just accepts the wasteful and dangerous assembly-line death factories that provide most of our protein. For that matter, it could be that this throwaway attitude has been deliberately fostered and supported by those leftover practices of a more barbaric age that we call the "meat processing" industry. That's a euphemism, of course, so we don't hurt our own feelings by thinking about all those dead animals.

Well, more of us need our feelings hurt so that we can save ourselves and our planet before it's too late. Read *The Jungle* by Upton Sinclair, which details the origins of the meat packing industry in the 1800s, and you may never eat meat again. Things have gotten better, but not as much as you might think.

If the horrors of the meat packing industry aren't enough to put you off your feed, then consider this: In a world as highly populated as the Earth, continuing to exploit animals for their resources is ecologically stupid. Forget fur harvesting, wool production, or raising animals just for draft, riding, racing, or hunting purposes. Livestock raising for food production is simply not sustainable in the long run. In fact, it has the potential to result in ecological catastrophe, whereas careful stewardship of the land by using it for farming food crops has a much greater potential for long-term sustainability and ecological health.

In this chapter, let's take a closer look at the effects that maintaining live-stock herds large enough to feed billions of people have on the only planet we know of that can sustain human life.

Home

Habitat Destruction

Large animals were not meant to be collected together in vast numbers in small areas, whether to breed or feed. Yes, there are exceptions: the seemingly endless bison herds on the Great Plains of colonial America, the caribou of the Far North, and the large migrations of wildebeest and other creatures in Africa. However, those examples were constrained by the carrying capacity of the land, and occurred only in times of plenty. In harder times, the harsh hand of nature trimmed their populations down to numbers capable of surviving on the limited resources available.

One of the hallmarks of humanity is that we have learned to manipulate our environment in ways that subvert natural processes for our benefit—at least for a while, and only if we're very careful to balance all the factors involved. If we don't, as William Butler Yeats so eloquently put it in the poem "The Second Coming," "things fall apart; the center cannot hold; mere anarchy is loosed upon the world." Though Yeats wrote that in response to the horrors of World War I, it's equally evocative of what usually happens as a result of raising animals for their own unnatural holocaust as a food source for selfish and uncaring humanity. Only those who do not "lack conviction," in Yeats's words, can change the environmental destruction that results from wanton misuse of nature's bounty.

You may have heard of "The Tragedy of the Commons." This describes events in medieval Europe when everyone allowed their livestock to graze on ground owned in common by everyone. Because no one person or group controlled it, anyone who was greedy or witless enough not to think ahead allowed the population of their livestock to grow so numerous that they stripped the land of more than their fair share of resources, whether it was grass or water. People acting according to their own self-interests instead of the common good ruined the land for everyone. The fact is, most people *do* think of their own self-interests first; it's human nature, left over from the every-family-for-itself days of our primitive ancestors. In any commons situation, someone will *always* take advantage, ruining the situation for everyone. We've seen this happen in every Communist country in the world. Consider the oligarchy that once controlled the old

Soviet Union with an iron fist, and the cult of personality that has developed around the ruler of North Korea, where famine is common but Dear Leader is

An inevitable Tragedy of the Commons result: depleted water supplies

never hungry. This is one of the better arguments for private ownership of land, but again, it serves as an illustration of environmental destruction due to overuse of said land. It's easy for large animals to exceed the carrying capacity of an area.

Since natural forces cannot act on livestock herds maintained and supported by humans, the result is the destruction of habitat. Anyone who has ever seen a sheep or goat pen where too many animals were kept has witnessed the results. The animals will literally eat the land bare of all vegetation, and then go to work on the trees as high as they can reach. The result looks like someone has taken hedge trimmers and trimmed all the trees to an even height above the ground, while the ground becomes bare dirt that is pounded to dust that blows away in the wind during dry weather, and is churned into mud that washes into the nearest streams during rainstorms.

These denuded areas don't necessarily stop at the edges of the animal pens. If the land within or near the pen is hilly, the bare ground may develop what geologists call "nick points" in the soil on the slopes, which can then develop into gullies very quickly—cutting across large tracts of land, widening and deepening with each heavy rain. On hillsides and mountainsides, these gullies—which lead inevitably to the nearest stream or river—can become up to ten feet deep, sometimes deeper. This erosion strips the land bare of topsoil, and sometimes subsoil if it continues unabated.

All these things together can make the land unlivable not just for domesticated animals, but for wild animals as well. Completely denuding the ground removes plants many herbivores need to survive, and declining herbivore populations removes the prey that carnivores need to survive. Even the insects who make those plants their homes, and the worms and grubs who live in the root systems of those plants, are lost. Whole ecosystems can collapse, at least locally.

The results of erosion: Sometimes beautiful, always barren

And what about all that soil that's lost? Obviously it goes somewhere, often causing damage to the environment where it ends up. Often it drifts on the wind to places tens or hundreds of miles away. In the summer of 2006, sandy soil stripped from plowed but unplanted fields in West Texas drifted away on strong winds and was dumped as far east as East Dallas, in Plano, Richardson, and Garland, not far from my home. It could have been much worse, and has been in the past. Poor agricultural practices, involving both plowing and overgrazing, resulted in the horrors of the Dust Bowl of the American Plains in the 1920s and 1930s. Witnesses report suffering through huge dust storms dozens of miles wide that could strip the paint off houses and automobiles, and might leave silt and sand up to several inches deep in buildings that were not properly sealed.

A 1930s Dust Bowl dust storm

Of course, agriculture continued in those areas later on, but with much greater care. Only now have the denuded areas really begun to recover, nearly a century later, and some say that recovery hasn't proceeded very far yet. That may be why so many areas aren't considered plantable in those regions—which leads to the argument that at least ranchers can "run cattle" or other animals that convert grass into edible food on that non-arable land. I find that to be a pretty circular argument.

A farm buried by Dust Bowl storms

The soil that isn't taken by the wind as "eolian" erosion goes with rain and other runoff in a process called "fluvial" or "alluvial" erosion. We can see this on a large-scale at the deltas of rivers like the Mississippi, where the silt and mud of a whole continent is dumped into the Gulf of Mexico. You also see it in the "alluvial fans" coming off mountain slopes. Over millions of years, this can transport materials as large as rocky cobbles hundreds or thousands of miles from their mountainous origins.

So it should be no surprise to realize that on a smaller scale, eroded soil often ends up in local waterways, where it sometimes clogs up the streams with mud and silt. Even when it doesn't, it may make the water undrinkable for wild animals, and decrease the oxygen content to the point where fish, crustacean, and other animals that depend on the aquatic ecology die in droves. Other imbalances can cause algae blooms that poison other things living in streams, ponds, and other bodies of water that receive too much of the eroded topsoil caused by animal husbandry and other failed agricultural practices—especially soil containing chemical fertilizers.

Out-of-control algae growth

Then there's the animal waste that goes into the watersheds along with the mud—or that's delivered deliberately into waterways from factory farms or slaughterhouses. I don't just mean fecal matter and urine. I've heard stories of waterways downstream of chicken processing plants where people had to stop swimming due to the presence of chicken blood and viscera floating in the water.

Some might argue that the fish in these streams will "clean up" such nastiness, but that's not necessarily so, and the decay products, while natural, can also poison the water if they're present in large quantities. Bacterial and algae blooms may also endanger lives and health. Remember, a lot of the water in these streams ends up in the groundwater that feeds aquifers and wells. Natural processes may filter out some of the pollutants as the water seeps through the soil and bedrock, but not all of them.

Even then, the pollutants remain in the soil and rock, and may be drawn into the groundwater and wells later on. Many of the particles are so small they percolate right through the natural filters of soil and bedrock to accumulate in the underground water supply. Bacteria, viruses, and prions are especially scary, especially prions, the barely-alive microbes that cause illnesses like Bovine Spongiform Encephalitis, otherwise known as mad cow disease. The same prions cause a similar disease in humans, literally poking holes in brain tissue.

Animal urine and feces contain uric acid, ammonia, and methane, all of which are natural, organic substances, but can be poisonous in large quantities. Just because something is "natural" and "organic" doesn't mean too much of it can't hurt you. Water is natural and organic too, but floods kill thousands of people every year, while just as many drown in accidents—and water isn't a nasty toxin like those listed above. The bottom line is that biological wastes in excess quantities are dangerous, because they are toxic and can breed and spread diseases. The same is true for unused animal remains—though there are few of those these days. Disgustingly, even chicken guts, bones, and brains are dried and ground up to feed other animals, when they're not converted into new petroleum in specialized plants—oil that we can burn to add even more toxins and pollutants to our atmosphere. Which brings us to my next argument.

Is it kind of warm lately, or is it just me?

Global Warming

The Earth exists in a delicate equilibrium that has persisted for millions, if not billions, of years. There are multitudes of climates and vegetation zones, based on what the land can naturally support considering elevation, latitude and longitude, the yearly amount of sunshine, and annual rainfall totals. Even the planet's atmospheric composition is well-balanced; too much of certain gases can trigger either ice ages or long periods of arid heat. While it's a bit more compli-

91

cated than that—we know, for example, that Earth's natural long-term wobble and the shape of its orbit around the sun also affect weather patterns over the eons, and the Sun has been steadily growing hotter for the last billion years— we've already seen what happens when too much water vapor and carbon dioxide fill the air: the climate changes. Some forecasters predict that summer days in Central and South Texas will get as high as 120° F in the next 10 years or so. I can only hope they're wrong! Whether this is our fault is up for debate; based on geo- logical research, some scientists point out that we're moving deeper into an "in- terstadial period," an epoch between Ice Ages, when it's normal for the weather to get that warm.

The last real ice age ended about 10,000 years ago, although we suffered a "Little Ice Age" from about A.D. 1400-1800. Remember hearing about the Dutch canals freezing in the old *Hans Brinker* story, or seeing the picture of Washing- ton crossing the Delaware in mid-winter, with the river full of floating icebergs? It rarely gets that cold either in Holland or Delaware these days. The Little Ice Age is one reason the Pilgrims had it so hard during their first few years in New England. Whatever the cause, it's hotter than it used to be on average, in the wake of the Industrial Revolution and our profligate use of fossil fuels, dumping mega- tons of carbon into the atmosphere every year. Plus, there are all those "hayburn- ers"—livestock—releasing their own global warming gas, methane, into the at- mosphere.

Yes, I *do* mean cow farts. Laugh it up, but it's a dangerous thing. Methane is a huge contributor to global warming. There are already more than 7.3 billion human beings contributing their share of methane to the atmosphere daily; the billions of animals we raise just to kill annually—especially cattle, which tend to be much larger than humans—produce at least as much methane. Most is broken

We dump billions of tons of greenhouse gases into the atmosphere annually

down by radiation in the upper atmosphere, but not before it helps trap a little more sunlight... and the amount is constantly replenished. In combination with increased carbon dioxide and water vapor, the two most common gases released when combustible fuels are burned, the methane seems to be slowly causing the average global temperature to rise to the point that polar ice caps have begun to melt. If this continues, global sea levels will rise significantly, drowning coastal communities and islands all over the world. A large percentage of the world's populations live on or near the coasts, or on low-lying islands that might, in time, be completely flooded.

While the Kevin Costner movie *Waterworld* was a tad over the top, if all the ice locked up in the ice caps and glaciers were to melt, the habitable land area of our world would decrease significantly. We've seen convincing evidence that this happened at the end of the last ice age, when melting ice sheets in the Northern Hemisphere not only drowned the thousand-mile-wide Bering Land Bridge connecting Asia and North America, but also adjusted many coastlines as much as a hundred miles or so inward. Florida, for example, used to be twice as wide as it is now.

This won't happen quickly, so there's still plenty of time to stop it. One way to do so is to start reducing our dependence on billions of meat, dairy, fur bearing, feather bearing, and laying animals, allowing their populations to decrease to more reasonable levels through attrition. Meanwhile, this will leave space for more plants to grow, reclaiming their old habitats. Reforestation—especially if we help it along—as well as an increased reliance on plant foods and products will inevitably improve the world as the planet literally becomes greener. More plant roots to hold the soil in place will reduce erosion, encourage topsoil formation, and aerate the soil. Dead plant matter will provide fertile humus, making the soil richer. Plants will inhale the extra carbon dioxide and exhale oxygen to help us all breathe, and many plant species can actually filter out pollution and fix it in the soil permanently, or in the case of larger plants and trees, in their own structures for long periods of time.

At the individual level, this process of healing the Earth is not all that difficult—even given the fact that most people won't participate, at least at first. All it takes is a few simple efforts, beginning with a determination to go Vegan. You don't even have to do it all at once. Just start eating more plant-based foods and using more plant-based products, from cotton clothes to wooden building materials, and that will naturally increase the demand for those products. In order to supply that demand, agricultural producers will have to shift their focus to plants. The need for meat and animal-supplied products like milk, cheese, fur, feathers, and wool will decrease. It's not necessary to stage a revolution to get this done.

We can just peacefully change our lifestyles, in ways that are so simple that you'll wonder why you didn't try them before.

We really can heal the world, one person at a time, if we stick to the strength of our convictions and convince other people to take the Vegan path. That's my goal with this book. Together, we can make a difference, conquer a staggering injustice, and make sure our species survives indefinitely.

You don't have to be Superman to save the world.

Chapter 5. Where Do We Go from Here?

If you've made it this far, I think we can agree that raising and harvesting animals just to eat them or to use their body products is a monumental waste and, in a way, one of humanity's most egregious sins. Even if you don't think that meat is murder, it's certainly a terrible perversion of the Biblical belief that we humans have dominion over all the beasts of the fields, the air, and the sea. Even if you believe that's true as part of your religion (and remember that many Vegans do not follow the Judeo-Christian belief system), nowhere does it say in holy texts that we should slaughter animals in their billions and pollute the planet in the process. In fact, as I recall it, the Bible urges that we do all things in moderation. We modern humans have not been moderate in our treatment of food animals, in the horror of the slaughterhouse, in our haste to render many species extinct, and in our rape of the seas.

Now, I'm not going to romanticize the ancients, or claim that they were conservationists in any way. Most were not; we have plenty of examples of them wasting resources, from the overloading of the carrying capacity of their homelands (e.g., the Mayans), to the Tragedy of the Commons, to bison jumps where Native Americans ran hundreds of animals over cliffs and then just slaughtered the ones they could reach, leaving the others to rot.

The problem here is numbers. As I've already pointed out, there are more than 7.3 billion humans in the world right this minute. Most of us eat meat, requiring the livestock and fishing industries to kill billions of animals per year to sate that hunger for animal protein. This process produces an extraordinary amount of waste, degrades the environment in ways not easily reversed, and worse, supports the attitude that it's acceptable to kill even when it's unnecessary to do so in order to survive. In this age of terrorism and weapons of mass destruction, is this something we should be teaching the next generations?

Will a transition to a Vegan society result in a more peaceful, more stable society? I may be biased, but I think it will. How many Vegans are likely to accept the murder of a human when they can't accept the murder of an animal? Although they may exist—there are eco-terrorists, after all—few Vegans are violent. We just want to be left alone, and want to leave the rest of the world alone, including the animals who share the planet with us. There is no need to raise animals just to exploit them, and no reason to hunt them, for that matter. We have alternative, and often cheaper, sources of food and other products than those produced by animals. We don't have to maintain these wasteful, degrading, horrifying practices anymore!

Yes, I have heard the arguments for hunting—that if animal populations were allowed to grow unchecked, there would be far too many animals, and they would be invading human properties in numbers impossible to control. It's already happening in some areas like semi-rural New Jersey or suburban San Antonio, Texas, where there are so many deer they cause car accidents and are referred to as "rats with antlers." But that argument holds only for hunting. First of all, would these animals be "moving in on our territory" looking for food if our rampant population growth and constant land hunger hadn't displaced them from *their* territory in the first place? Probably not.

Second, this is a temporary situation. As harsh as Mother Nature is, in time the overpopulation we see today will result in a dieback among the animal populations, until only the number the existing land can support will survive. In the meantime, we can drive more carefully, build fences around our yards, plant flowers that deer refuse to eat (and there are many), and be responsible stewards of our children and pets for once, protecting them from predators like coyotes. There are also humane ways to handle the population explosions, if only by trapping the animals and moving them into wilderness areas, or finding ways to sterilize them so the populations drop quickly. We did it with the screwflies in California in just a few years several decades ago. The reason most of us aren't willing to do these things is because they cost more money than just giving hunters permits to kill the animals, and no one wants to spend that money.

Well, isn't that money worth spending if we can raise generations of children with greater respect for life, both human and otherwise?

And let's get real here. Even if we ignore the ethical arguments for Veganism (which I think is a serious mistake), the only way we're going to maintain our population and standard of living is by converting to a largely vegetarian, if not entirely Vegan, diet. Aside from the fact that they occupy areas that we can use for other things, maintaining huge herds of animals of any type is going to continue to degrade our land, pollute the streams, rivers, lakes, oceans, and groundwater, and make the air harder to breathe. The methane and water vapor generated by large animals (including us!) is contributing to global climate change. Think about all the horrific flooding in some parts of the United States this past decade (most recently in southwest Louisiana), while others have been baking in years-long droughts. Until a couple of years ago, the droughts in the Southwest were so bad that some of the reservoirs we depend on for water here in Texas practically dried up. Do you remember these oddball weather patterns ten, fifteen, twenty years ago? There have always been extremes, but my research suggests that the rainfall patterns have changed drastically in many parts of the U.S. alone in the last couple of decades. The summers are getting hotter; month-long periods of 100-degree highs are not uncommon in Texas in the summer, and daily highs from 105-110 degrees occur multiple times each year.

Coincidence? Or are we to blame? Even though the hole in the ozone seems to be healing now that we're no longer using chlorofluorocarbons, it's still too hot. For many of us in the Southwest, the winter of 2015-2016 was barely a winter at all, with few days below freezing in Central and South Texas. It was literally colder in April 2016 than in January.

Given the frequency of bright, sunny, cloudless days, it may be time to invest in solar panels to power your home... if you're not worried about them being shattered by unseasonable hailstorms, like the ones in Texas in April 2016 that shot softball-sized hailstones at us like they were fired out of cannons, shattering windows, auto windshields, and skylights, and leaving roofs, trailer homes, and manufactured homes looking like Swiss cheese. As of this writing in December 2016, the insurance companies still haven't finished processing all the claims—and some law firms are making fortunes suing them for slow or denied claims.

We can't continue to foul our nest and knowingly stunt our own ethical evolution. Even if we had a million planets like Earth we could move to, it would still be a terrible waste. Even renewable resources take a long time to renew, no matter how advanced our technology gets.

We need to make plants a much bigger part of our lives.

I'm optimistic that we as a species are now slowly learning to control ourselves and help conserve what we have. While we're far from perfect, from what I can tell, things are generally better than they were 30-40 years ago in terms of pollution. We're recycling more, we use much more biodegradable packaging and containers, we're more careful with the land, we're finding new ways to convert pollution like carbon in the atmosphere and chicken remains into useable materials—even energy sources—and we've increased reforestation efforts. We're also finding new, nonpolluting energy sources to use—and more and more of us are adopting Veganism and vegetarianism as a lifestyle.

As a result, many of our lakes and bays are clearing up, smog has become less of a problem, and we're slowly decreasing the number of animals killed per capita for our diet. As that number goes down, the nasty by-products of the meat-processing and animal husbandry industry, from erosion and environmental poisoning to damage to our ethical development, are sure to decrease significantly. This world will become, more and more, one that we want to live in and leave to our descendants.

But make no mistake, this is only a start! By no means are we perfect, even if we *are* getting better. We have to keep it up, and push even harder as more and more people join us on "Spaceship Earth." We have to make sure that we use every little thing plants can give us when we harvest them, right down to the fibers that we can use for clothing, mats, and other things. Nothing can go to waste.

A Teenager's Efforts to Save the World

Some people may think I'm naïve about my belief that Veganism can cure many of the world's ills, and maybe I am. If I had lived 150 or even 100 years ago, I probably wouldn't even have thought twice about what I was eating, or about all the waste and suffering that went into it. My parents might have even owned a farm back then, as so many families did at the time. Honestly, there really wasn't that much of an option in terms of alternatives for foods and some of the animal-based materials we use now; rubber was uncommon, and plastics weren't in wide use until after WWI. Milk came from cows and goats, and so did cheese and butter (though there was some really nasty margarine available in some places that was basically axle grease). Back then, people even still used sheep entrails for stringing their tennis rackets, and many balls were literally made from animal bladders sheathed in animal skin.

To borrow a famous book title from S.E. Hinton, That Was Then; This Is Now. We can make great-tasting milk from soybeans and almonds that we can use for everything people use cow milk for, except churn butter and make cheese. Those products can be made in delicious varieties from nut milks, enzymes, and salt. We more fully understand our nutritional requirements and the nutritional values of almost everything we eat, so we know how to find and easily get the protein, fats, and carbohydrates we need to stay healthy. Nutritional supplements are common and easily acquired. The Internet makes it easy to buy anything that's not available in local stores, and it doesn't have to be that expensive!

If you absolutely need the texture of meat, you can get it from Textured Vegetable Protein, mostly pea and soy protein. Fake but tasty eggs are available if you need them. Plastics and rubber have replaced leather and other animal skins and innards in almost everything. Fertilizers can be made from chemicals, not ground-up animal bones, dried blood, and manure. Old soda bottles can be made into cheap fleece just as soft and warm as a lamb's.

We don't have to kill and exploit animals any more, either for food or the other products of their bodies. Because of that, we can make this world a healthier, better, safer place to live.

That's worth fighting for, no matter how "naïve" or "idealistic" people think you are. And it's really the only way we're going to keep evolving and growing as a culture, especially as our population continues to increase.

That's the reason I founded my blog *My Vegan Dreams,* as well as my Facebook, Instagram, and Twitter accounts of the same name. Another great thing about living in the 21st century is social media! Anyone with a computer can reach out and start changing the world for the better, touching people's lives all around the world. I feel I've done that with my sites, which is another reason why I've written this book—to increase my presence even more, in venues that people who don't participate as much in social media can have easy access to. I have an acquaintance who says he "fails at Facebook" because he doesn't take the time to check it every day. This book is one way to reach people like him, people who are sickened by the waste, hypocrisy, and horror of the meat production industry but don't know where to turn for more information, or for tips on how to help.

Another way I plan to reach out to others while helping the planet is through my brand-new clothing line, Project Let Live. The goals of this project are to protect farm animals from cruelty, inspire people to look at and treat animals in a more compassionate way, and to give back to organizations that are making the biggest impact to help save innocent animals' lives. I will be donating 10% of the proceeds to farm sanctuaries. Keep an eye on my social media for more news on that front!

My main website, http://myVegandreams.com/, is where I do most of my writing. I maintain the blog, write articles (one popular one is about where Vegans get their protein), review yummy Vegan products, and even have a counter that keeps track of how many animals have been killed for food or their body products since you opened the site. You'll surely be appalled at how quickly the numbers climb! I include articles on health, Vegan products, lifestyle, and products I personally love. Veganism is actually a pretty vibrant lifestyle with a wonderful community where people are eager to help out each other and the world. We're not the insufferable self-righteous prudes some people think we are. We're just really serious about making this world a better place, one rescued animal at a time. If I can get only one person to start eating kale rather than veal, I've served my purpose.

Now, I've already mentioned that my Mom and Dad are Internet marketing whizzes, so they knew exactly what to show me to help me make the very best sites possible. Mom, as a diehard Vegan now, even contributes to the business. But I do most of the content, including the videos, responding to my audience's comments and questions and taking care of the site. I am proud to say that

I have had many hundreds of thousands of hits, and I have well over 170,000 followers as of writing this on my Facebook Page which can be found at http://facebook.com/myVegandreams. My goal, as I note on my Facebook Page, is to inspire young and old around the world that Veganism is the best way of life.

As I go on to say, "I am Vegan for the people, the planet, and the animals. I made this page to support you in your Vegan journey. I realize everyone has a different view that is personal to them on what it means to be Vegan. Many factors come into play: availability, budget, demographics, family, beliefs, health, etc.... So my message and mission here is to support you no matter what your choices are and no matter where you are in your journey."

That's partly my goal with this book as well, but to be honest, I wrote it largely to explain why a meat-eating lifestyle is so horrible for all of us and our world, and to counter the most common myths about Veganism and related lifestyles. We Vegans are not eco-terrorists. We are not out to make you feel bad about yourself or to undermine your traditions. But we aren't going to hide from the truth like so many people do these days. It's a fact that you can eat well, stay healthy, and live a good, long life by being a Vegan. It's not even hard anymore if you have access to a computer. If you can spend money on corn dogs, cheese fries, and pork chops, you can afford to buy green vegetables, fruits, vegetable protein, and any supplements you need. If you can't find the right foods in your local stores, know that you can find them online. It's not hard. You can even find alternate foods in most restaurants, especially in big cities.

There are no more excuses not to become Vegan, except a lack of will. If a teenager can do it—and can attract a worldwide following without being a crazy militant type—then you can do it too! And I encourage you to do so. Accept the challenge of a lifetime!

If you're worried about what kinds of dishes to prepare, don't be. In the appendix, I'm going to include a complete updated copy of my cookbook, "30 Easy Vegan Recipes." Not only will I discuss how to balance your diet for maximum health, I'll provide great recipes for breakfast, lunch, and dinner. No matter who you are or your health needs, there are delicious Vegan foods for you to eat, foods that make eating a joy, not a chore. And no longer will you have to worry about lactose intolerance, gout, hardening of the arteries, or many other food-related illnesses that can be traced to eating meat. All that is wiped away utterly by a Vegan diet.

So let's get our Vegan on, shall we?

Here's where you can connect with me!

http://instagram.com/my_Vegan_dreams

http://twitter.com/my_Vegan_dreams

http://myVegandreams.com

http://facebook.com/myVegandreams

APPENDIX: 30 Easy Vegan Recipes

MY VEGAN DREAMS

30 EASY VEGAN RECIPES

RECIPES & REFERENCE GUIDE

MEGAN ALPHA

What IS Vegan Cooking?

Simply put, Vegan cooking is simply preparing foods that contain NO animal products. Cooking Vegan is environmentally friendly, animal friendly and not to mention it's really good for you!

So, What Does It Mean to Be Vegan?

First let me state that being Vegan is different from vegetarian. Vegetarians still drink milk and/or eat eggs. Vegans do not. In fact, for most Vegans, being Vegan is not just a health choice but also an ethical choice. It's a way of life, called Veganism.

When first starting out Vegan, it can be challenging to find prepared meals because eggs and milk, for example, are common baking ingredients. Therefore, in order to follow a Vegan diet, substitutions need to be made.

What Makes Food Vegan or Not?

When striving for a Vegan diet it's important to note that there are a lot of hidden ingredients in many of the foods that we consume. Therefore, if you are going for a strict Vegan diet there are some important things you should watch out for.

- Vegans don't eat animal products or byproducts of animals.
- They also don't consume things like milk and eggs.
- Vegans also don't eat fish.
- Bees are animals so Vegans also don't eat honey, royal jelly, nor take bee pollen supplements.
- There are also plenty of hidden ingredients to look out for that tend to make their way into food including gelatin, lard, palm oil (unsustainable) and whey.

If you are a new Vegan, making all of these changes at once may seem overwhelming. But, with time and education becoming Vegan will eventually be an easy journey.

What This Appendix Will Cover

- Common non-Vegan ingredients that can be substituted with Vegan ingredients.
- A list of typical ingredients used in Vegan cooking.
- A list of hidden ingredients to avoid while eating a Vegan diet.
- Information on how to stock a complete Vegan pantry so you can prepare Vegan dishes every day without a hassle.
- Getting the right balance of vitamins, minerals, and nutrients for your body.
- Recipes so you can get started cooking right away.

As you can see, there's a lot of information to take in on how to enjoy a Vegan diet. This Appendix is designed to teach you everything you need to know.

Typical Ingredients

As I mentioned above, Vegan cooking is cooking without animal products, that means meat, fish, eggs, or byproducts of any of these things.

When I first started out Vegan I noticed that eggs & milk were in a lot of baked goods. Therefore, that led me to start doing my own cooking and finding simple replacements for eggs & milk that were Vegan.

This section will focus on several different kinds of ingredients that you can replace with a Vegan option.

Egg Replacement Options

Eggs basically bind ingredients together. They can provide moisture, make ingredients light and fluffy and also help baked goods rise. You will find that most baked good recipes call for eggs; therefore, below you will find some egg replacement options. Replacing eggs in a recipe doesn't have to be challenging. There are many options in today's market to choose from.

Pureed Bananas

Using 1/2 of a ripe banana is equivalent to one egg. Place a banana in a blender and turn it into a puree to replace your egg in any recipe.

Ground Flaxseeds

One tablespoon of finely ground flaxseed with 3 tablespoons of water will replace one egg. Flaxseeds have a nutty taste so this egg replacement works best with muffins and pancakes.

Egg Replacement Product

A quick and convenient way to replace eggs in your recipe is to keep and egg replacement powder on hand from your local grocery store or purchase online. Just make sure you read the ingredients to make sure it is Vegan friendly. There are definitely several different egg replacement products on the market so test a few out and see which one you prefer.

Tofu as an Egg Replacement

Silken Tofu is another option. Make sure you buy organic non-GMO tofu. I have seen a lot of tofu on the market that is not GMO free. Tofu blends nicely with most flavors. Tofu really doesn't have a flavor, so it typically takes on the flavors of your cooking.

To replace one large egg, use ¼ cup of blended tofu.

Using Flour and Other Leavening Agents

Making pastes from different flours and leavening agents is another option for replacing egg. The advantage to using flour or a leavening agent is that you don't have the additional flavor that you would have if you used a banana or flaxseed. Here are some options:

- 1 tablespoon flour of any kind (organic wheat flour, organic oat flour, or organic soy flour) and 1 tablespoon water for each egg.
- 1 tablespoon baking powder, 1 tablespoon organic flour, 2 tablespoons water for each egg.
- 2 tablespoons cornstarch and 2 tablespoons water blended together also replaces one egg.

Finding the Right Egg Substitute

Finding the right egg substitute just requires a little bit of experimentation to find the best one for your cooking needs. With each recipe you cook to replace eggs with one of the above suggestions, you will find which one results in the desired taste and consistency that you prefer.

Replacing Milk in Recipes

Vegans do NOT drink any kind of milk that comes from an animal such as sheep, cow, goat, etc... Milk is another very common ingredient you will find in most recipes. The good news is replacing milk is pretty easy, just replace 1 cup of milk with 1 cup of your Vegan alternative.

Here's a List of Vegan Alternatives:

- ***Soy milk*** - Soy milk can be found in most grocery stores and soy milk comes in a variety of flavors from different companies. Flavors include vanilla, unsweetened, chocolate, and even egg nog. You will find that soy milk is rich in protein and some brands tend to be creamier than others.

Test out a few if you decide to go with soy milk to find the best alternative for your cooking needs.

- ***Nut milks*** - My personal favorite is almond milk and just like soy milk, almond milk comes in a variety of flavors. You can also use cashew milk and hazelnut milk as another option. Most nut milks come in different flavors and also come in sweetened and unsweetened.
- ***Rice milk*** - Rice milk is another great option but if you are looking for additional protein, rice milk is low on protein.
- ***Hemp milk*** - Hemp milk, or hemp seed milk, is a plant milk made from hemp seeds that are soaked and ground in water, yielding a beany-nutty cream-flavored substance. There are various options available such as organic, non-GMO and conventional along with unsweetened, original, vanilla and chocolate flavored.

As you become familiar with the different flavors of milk replacement products, you'll start to get a taste for which one you prefer.

Replacing Buttermilk in Recipes

From time to time you may also find buttermilk as a requirement in some recipes. Buttermilk is also an animal product that is basically just milk that has been cultured.

Here's how to make your own Vegan-friendly Buttermilk:

1. Measure one cup of soy milk in a glass measuring cup.
2. Add 1 tablespoon of vinegar or apple cider vinegar or lemon juice and mix together.
3. Let it sit for about ten minutes before using it.

Soy milk works the best and rice milk and nut milks don't work as well. The chemistry of soy milk is better suited for a replacement.

Replacing Butter

Butter is another common ingredient that a lot of recipes call for. Here are some options you can use to substitute butter.

- **Earth Balance Products -** Most would just reach for margarine but I recommend using a non-hydrogenated butter substitute such as products from Earth Balance.
- **Shortening -** Vegetable shortening can also be used. One tablespoon of shortening is equivalent to 1 tablespoon of butter.
- **Oils -** Oils such as coconut oil, olive oil, and grapeseed oil can also be substituted for butter. One tablespoon of oil is equivalent to 1 tablespoon of butter.

Common Ingredients Used in Vegan Cooking

Having a well-stocked kitchen equipped with Vegan ingredients can save you a lot of time. Over the years, I have found there are some common ingredients and foods that we use quite often so we always try and keep these items in our refrigerator or pantry.

Here's a rundown of some of the most common:

- Dairy free milk
- Tofu
- Tempeh
- Seitan
- Jackfruit
- Vegan butter such as Earth Balance

- Meat alternatives
- Dairy free yogurt
- Miso
- Tamari
- Tahini
- Braggs Aminos
- Braggs Apple Cider Vinegar
- Dairy free cheese
- Nut butter (almond butter, peanut butter, cashew butter, etc.)
- Vegan bread
- Bee Free Honee
- Egg replacement
- Extra Virgin Coconut Oil
- Extra Virgin Olive Oil
- Cumin powder
- Curry powder
- Thyme
- Oregano
- Basil
- Garlic powder
- Himalayan salt
- Ground pepper
- Cane Sugar
- Agave nectar
- Nuts / Seeds (almonds, cashews, pumpkin seeds, walnuts, pecans, etc.)
- Beans (Garbanzo, black beans, kidney beans, lentils, etc.)
- Pasta
- Risotto
- Rice
- Quinoa

- Oats
- Nutritional Yeast
- Dried fruits (raisins, cranberries, figs, apricots, etc.)
- Organic Fruits
- Organic Vegetables

Being Vegan is a plant based diet so make sure you keep a variety of colors when it comes to fruits and vegetables on hand so you get the necessary vitamins, minerals, and nutrients on a daily basis.

Always look for organic produce whenever possible and look for non-GMO products. If you can't find fresh organic produce due to the season, then look for a variety of organic fruits and vegetables in the frozen section of your favorite store.

Being Vegan doesn't mean you have to cook everything. With more awareness of Veganism many stores carry already prepared Vegan foods.

Here are a few ideas you could look for at your local grocery store:

- Vegan desserts
- Vegan baked goods
- Vegan pancake mix
- Vegan frozen snacks
- Vegan ice cream
- Vegan snacks
- Vegan chocolate
- Vegan crackers
- Vegan chips
- Vegan cereals
- Vegan bread
- Vegan meat alternatives

Here are a few of our favorite brands:

- Gardein Products (frozen section)
- Earth Balance
- Skinny Pop Popcorn
- One Degree Organic Cereals
- Barbara Breakfast Cereals
- NuGo Vegan protein bars
- Boca veggie nuggets
- Vegan Amy's Pizza
- Daiya Vegan Cheese
- Daiya Vegan Pizza
- Daiya Yogurt
- Go Raw Sprouted Cookies
- Vegan Egg by Follow Your Heart
- Steady Eddie Bread
- Divvies Cookies
- Sky Valley Peanut Sauce and Sriracha
- Vegenaise
- Beyond Meat Products
- Dr. Praeger's Veggie Burgers
- Sweet Earth Veggie Bacon
- Upton Products (seitan & jackfruit)
- Sweet Earth (breakfast & lunch burritos)

These are just a few examples, but there are a lot of products on the market that are Vegan but not necessarily labeled Vegan. We call this accidently Vegan.

http://www.peta.org/accidentallyVegan/

NOTE: A lot of those products on that list are NOT healthy, but we wanted to give you some additional resources.

Hidden Ingredients to Watch For

We talked a bit about some hidden ingredients earlier, but in this section, we are going to go into more detail. As a Vegan, you will want to avoid these hidden ingredients and become more familiar with what you are looking for when looking at the ingredients on food labels. If the package is labeled VEGAN, you can be fairly confident all ingredients are Vegan. Though there may come a time when you are looking at a food label and the product is not labeled Vegan and you want to do a quick check before eating.

Hidden Ingredients That Are Animal Products:

- Albumin - comes from egg whites
- Milk products - includes whey protein powder, lactase, lactose, and things like milk and dried milk
- Calcium Caseinate – is a protein produced from casein in skim and sometimes 1% milk
- Calcium Stearate – also another additive obtained from animal sources
- Suet – a type of animal fat
- Tallow – animal fat product is made from suet
- Bee products – This includes royal jelly, propolis, honey, and bee pollen
- Carmine – a food additive that comes from insects
- Lard – a type of animal fat
- Casein – this is the protein that is in cheese
- Gelatin – from animals, a popular product found especially in jellies and desserts
- Cochineal - from bugs
- Isinglass - fish byproduct
- Muristic acid - from animals
- Oleic acid - from animals
- Palmitic acid - fatty acid found in animals
- Pancreatin - found in animals

- Pepsin - derived from pigs
- Palm Oil that is NOT from a sustainable source

The point in sharing all these ingredients is that there will be a time when you may want to grab something on the go. You may be considering a product that isn't labeled Vegan, and having this list is a great way to stay loyal to Veganism.

Kitchen Equipment

Once I started cooking Vegan recipes on a regular basis I found that there were some essential kitchen items I used on a regular basis I thought I would share with you.

Kitchen Equipment List:
- Quinoa cooker
- Rice cooker
- Wok
- Quinoa strainer
- Pasta strainer
- Food Processor (we use a Vitamix)
- Casserole dishes
- Glass storage containers
- 8qt. Stockpot
- Stainless steel pots and pans (variety of sizes)
- Toaster
- Crockpot
- Baking sheets
- Loaf pans
- Muffin pans
- Cutting board

- Knives
- Utensils
- Glass measuring cups
- Measuring spoons
- Vegetable peeler
- Whisk

Nutritional Considerations

This section will cover some of the challenges Vegans face when eating Vegan. I want to help you create healthy and balanced meal combinations that will leave you full of energy and health. If you want to lose weight or stay thin, just remember not to consume too many calories in addition.

Getting Adequate Protein

People who eat meat always ask us Vegans where do we get our protein from? You don't have to be a meat eater to get protein. In fact, most meat eaters are also getting their protein from the same plant sources Vegans eat. Here are products in the plant world that are rich in protein:

- Soy protein
- Nuts, seeds, nut milk, nut butters
- Grains, especially quinoa
- Legumes
- Plant based protein drinks (remember whey is not Vegan, look for plant based protein mixes)

Iron

For many women, being Vegan can cause an iron deficiency so check with your doctor to see if you need to take an iron supplement.

Here are some foods rich in iron:

- Spinach
- Green beans
- Brewer's yeast
- Wheat germ
- Lima beans
- Dried fruit such as raisins and prunes
- Blackstrap molasses
- Fortified iron products (orange juice)

B-Vitamins

Vegans typically get enough B vitamins, but B12 is the more challenging vitamin. Here are some ways to get more B12 (again consult with your doctor to see if you need more B12 in your diet):

- Fortified B12 cereals
- Nutritional yeast (Braggs)
- Fortified B12 plant milks
- My kind B12 daily spray

Favorite Vegan Mobile Apps

Before we dive into the recipes, I want to share with you some of my favorite mobile apps that help with my Vegan journey, especially while travelling. You can find these apps in your app store on your smart phone by simply searching the name.

- **Is it Vegan** - use this app to scan foods that have bar codes to determine if it's Vegan.

- **Happy Cow** - need to find Vegan places to eat while travelling? Happy Cow is an app that locates the nearest Vegan - vegetarian-friendly establishments in your area.
- **Peta** - stay up to date with what's happening in the Vegan world such as new products and news.
- **Bunny Free** - this app provides a list of companies that are cruelty free
- **Animal Free** - this app provides a massive list of those hidden ingredients that are not free of animal products
- **VeganXpress** - an app that provides menu & Vegan shopping assistance
- **Cruelty Free** - this app provides a list of all US and Canada companies that do not test their ingredients, formulations or finished products on animals.

Collection of Our Favorite Recipes

Now, it's time to put it all together and try some new recipes. This section gives you a sampling of some of the recipes you can prepare on a Vegan diet. Feel free to adapt and change them as you see fit.

Everyone's tastes differ and you may also want to change things around, depending on your mood or what you have on hand.

Breakfast Recipes

Tofu Scramble

<u>Ingredients:</u>

- 1 tbsp. olive oil
- 3 potatoes, cubed
- ¼ red onion, minced
- 1 red bell pepper, chopped
- 1 green bell pepper, chopped
- 1 block extra-firm tofu, drained
- 1 tbsp. nutritional yeast
- ½ tsp. oregano
- ½ tsp. garlic powder
- ½ tsp. ground coriander

- ½ tsp. ground cumin
- ½ tsp. black pepper
- ½ tsp. salt
- ½ tsp. turmeric
- ½ tsp. garlic powder
- ¼ cup water
- 1 large tomato, diced
- 4-6 cups spinach, chopped
- 1 avocado, peeled and sliced
- Salsa (optional)

Instructions:

1. Put cubed potatoes in a pot of boiling water. Cook until tender then set aside.

2. Heat oil in a large sauté pan on medium high. Add potatoes and cook until brown. Add onion, peppers and cook until onions and peppers are softened, about 5 minutes.

3. Add tofu by crumbling into pan with potatoes, onions and peppers.

4. While the mixture is cooking prepare spice mixture in a small glass bowl. Combine nutritional yeast, oregano, turmeric, garlic powder, ground coriander, ground cumin, salt and pepper, mix together.

3. Add spice mixture to the pan with the tofu, potatoes, and peppers mixing well. Add water to help mix spices within the dish.

4. Turn off heat from the stove and fold in chopped tomato and chopped spinach until spinach starts to wilt.

5. Transfer scramble to a bowl. Top with avocado and/or salsa. You can also use mixture to wrap up in a Vegan tortilla. Enjoy!

Oatmeal Power Bowl

Ingredients:

- ⅓ c organic rolled oats
- ⅔ c Almond milk or nut milk of your choice
- 1 scoop chocolate or vanilla Vegan protein powder of your choice
- 1 tbsp. organic chia seeds
- 1 ripe banana sliced
- Handful of blueberries

Instructions :

Mix together the night before in a glass container oats, chia seeds, and almond milk, cover and refrigerator overnight. In the morning add either vanilla or chocolate protein powder and additional milk if needed to desired consistency. Top sliced bananas and blueberries. Enjoy!

Easy Fruit Yogurt Bowl

Ingredients:

- Vanilla dairy-free yogurt (Coconut yogurt, Daiya or Kite Hill, etc.)
- ¼ c granola (buy a Vegan brand or make your own *recipe below)
- ½ banana
- Handful of blueberries
- 3-4 sliced strawberries

Instructions:

Put yogurt from container into a breakfast bowl. Mix in granola, banana, blueberries and strawberries. Grab a spoon and enjoy!

*Homemade Granola

Ingredients:

- 3 ½ cups of organic rolled oats
- 1 c nuts of choice

• 1 c dried fruit of choice (raisins, cranberries, etc.)

• 3 tbsp. seeds of choice

• 1 tbsp. ground cinnamon

• 1 tsp. salt

• 1 tbsp. vanilla extract

• ¼ c grapeseed oil

• ¼ c agave nectar or bee free honee

Instructions:

1. Preheat oven to 325 degrees Fahrenheit. Line a large baking sheet with parchment paper.
2. Combine all ingredients in a large bowl, mixing together.
3. Spread mix on baking sheet put in oven for 10 minutes. Stir then bake an additional 10-15 minutes. Watch closely that it does not burn.
4. Let cool and put in an airtight container.

Whole Wheat Chocolate Chip Banana Pancakes

Ingredients:

• 2 ½ cups whole wheat pastry flour or all-purpose flour

• 2 tbsp. white cane sugar

• 2 tsp. baking soda

• ½ tsp. salt

• 2 cups non-dairy milk

• ½ tsp. vanilla extract

• 1 small mashed banana (optional)

• Vegan chocolate chips (optional) (such as Enjoy Life semi-sweet chocolate chips)

Instructions:

1. In a large bowl, mix together flour, sugar, baking soda, salt.
2. Add in slowly while mixing non-dairy milk, mashed banana, and vanilla extract till there are no more dry spots.
3. Heat a skillet or griddle on medium heat. Lightly grease skillet. Pour a small amount onto skillet to form a pancake. Cook for 2 minutes on one side or until you see bubbles. Flip pancakes and add a few chocolate chips to the top of the pancake and push chips down into pancake with spatula. Once pancake looks golden brown remove and repeat the process until you are done making your batch of pancakes.
4. Let cool and grab a fork! Enjoy!

Banana French Toast

Ingredients:

- 1 ripe banana
- 1 ¼ cups of unsweetened almond milk
- ½ tbsp. chia seed
- ¼ tsp. cinnamon
- 4 - 5 slices bread
- ½ tsp. vanilla extract
- Maple syrup

Instructions:

1. Mash banana in a large bowl.
2. Add almond milk, chia seeds, cinnamon, vanilla and stir. If batter appears too thick, just add more almond milk.
3. Preheat your griddle or skillet to medium heat.
4. Spread Vegan butter such as Earth Balance generously across griddle or use coconut oil.

5. Dip slices of bread in mixture and soak well on both sides. Transfer soaked bread to griddle and cook evenly on both sides until golden brown.
6. Serve with your favorite Vegan toppings, or maple syrup. Enjoy!

Vegan Egg McMuffin

Ingredients:

- 1 tbsp. of olive oil
- 2 level Tablespoons of Vegan Egg (we use Follow Your Heart)
- ½ c of iced cold water
- 2 pieces of Vegan bacon (we use Sweet Earth)
- 2 tbsp. Daiya shredded cheese
- Vegan English muffin

Instructions:

1. Whisk Vegan egg powder and Daiya cheese with ice cold water. Heat egg pan to medium heat along with olive oil and cook Vegan egg till done flipping a few times. Remove egg from pan.
2. Toast English muffin in a toaster and place on a plate when toasted.
3. Add Vegan egg to ½ of the English muffin.
4. Cook Vegan bacon according to instructions. When done remove from heat and add to the top of the Vegan egg.
5. Close English muffin into a sandwich.
6. Grab a napkin and enjoy!

Cinnamon Quinoa Bowl

Ingredients:

- 1 c water
- 1 c almond milk or dairy free milk

- 1 c organic red and white quinoa
- 1 cup organic raspberries
- 1 cup organic blackberries
- ½ tsp. ground cinnamon
- ⅓ c pepita seeds or substitute with a seed of your choice
- 4 tsp. bee free honee or agave nectar

Instructions:

1. Combine dairy free milk, and quinoa in a medium saucepan. Bring to a boil over medium to high heat. Reduce heat to medium low and cover to simmer.
2. Once quinoa has absorbed liquid and is done add raspberries, blackberries, agave nectar of bee free honey and cinnamon.
3. Top with seeds.
4. Grab your spoon and enjoy!

Chocolate Banana Smoothie

Ingredients:

- ½ c dairy free vanilla yogurt
- 1 c dairy free cold milk
- 1 frozen banana
- 1 scoop of chocolate Vegan protein powder

Instructions:

Mix all ingredients in a blender until smooth. Serve cold and with a straw. Enjoy!

Yummy Smoothie Bowl

Ingredients:

- 1 c almond milk
- ½ frozen banana
- ½ c organic frozen mixed berries

Toppings:

- Handful blueberries
- Handful raspberries
- Handful blackberries
- Handful of Vegan granola

Instructions:

1. Blend together almond milk, frozen banana and mixed berries in a blender till blended.
2. Pour contents into a bowl and top with blueberries, raspberries, Vegan granola, and blackberries.
3. Grab a spoon and enjoy!

Banana Chia Pudding

Ingredients:

- ¼ c chia seeds
- 1 c of light or regular coconut milk
- ½ tsp. of agave nectar or bee free honee
- ½ banana
- Handful of pepita seeds or pumpkin seeds

Instructions:

1. Mix chia seeds, coconut milk, and agave nectar in a glass mason jar. Refrigerate overnight.

2. Remove from fridge next morning. Make sure the pudding looks thick and the chia seeds have gelled together.

3. Top with fresh bananas and pepita seeds.

4. Grab a spoon and enjoy!

Lunch Recipes

Avocado Toast with Sriracha

Ingredients:

- 2 pieces of Vegan bread
- 1 large avocado
- Sriracha
- Salt and Pepper

Instructions:

1. Toast bread in toaster and place on a plate when toasted.
2. Mash avocado in a glass bowl.
3. Mix in sriracha, salt & pepper to your liking.
4. Spread mixture across both pieces of toast and enjoy!

Vegan BLT

Ingredients:

- Vegan bread two pieces
- 4 slices plant based bacon (we use Sweet Earth Benevolent Bacon)
- Romaine lettuce chopped
- Avocado sliced
- 1 Tomato sliced
- Vegenaise or Hummus (optional)

Instructions:

1. Toast your bread in a toaster and set aside on a plate.
2. Add Vegenaise or hummus to your sandwich as a spread.
3. Cook plant based bacon according to packaging instructions.
4. Once done it's time to build your sandwich. Add lettuce, avocado, tomato and cooked bacon.
5. Grab a napkin and enjoy!

Quinoa Salad with Cucumber, Red Onion & Beans

Ingredients:

- 2 c quinoa
- 1 - 14 oz can of Garbanzo beans
- 1 - 14 oz can of Black beans
- 1 c cilantro, finely chopped
- 1 c parsley, finely chopped
- 1 red onion, chopped
- 1 cucumber, diced
- 10 - 15 cherry tomatoes cut in halves
- 3 celery stalks, finely chopped

- 3 tbsp. pine nuts
- ½ c Dill, finely chopped
- Salt and Pepper
- Braggs Aminos

Instructions:

1. Cook quinoa according to directions. Set aside when done.
2. While quinoa is cooking heat Garbanzo and Black beans together on medium heat. Once tender drain and rinse.
3. Put beans in a large bowl and add cilantro, parsley, onion, cucumber, tomatoes, celery, pine nuts, dill and mix together.
4. Fold in quinoa until mixed evenly.
5. Salt and Pepper as needed.
6. Add in Braggs Aminos for desired taste.

Avocado & White Bean Club

Ingredients:

- 2 - 15 oz white beans, rinsed and drained
- 2 tbsp. extra-virgin olive oil
- ½ tsp. Himalayan salt
- ½ tsp. black pepper
- Vegan bread
- 1 red onion, thinly sliced
- 1 cucumber, thinly sliced
- 1 4-5 oz container of your favorite sprouts
- 1 avocado, sliced

Instructions:

1. In a medium bowl, combine the beans, oil, salt, and pepper. Mash the mixture until mostly smooth.
2. Toast 2 slices of bread. Spread mixture on both sides of the bread.
3. Add cucumber, onion, sprouts, and avocado to one side and close sandwich with remainder piece of bread.
4. Slice sandwich in half and enjoy!

Hummus Tortilla Pizza

Ingredients:

- 10" whole grain tortilla or bigger
- ⅓ - ½ c Vegan hummus
- ½ c fresh basil, chopped
- 7 cherry tomatoes, sliced
- ½ c spinach, chopped
- Kalamata olives
- Add other veggies (optional)
- Nutritional yeast

Instructions:

1. Preheat oven to 400 degrees F.
2. Line pizza pan with parchment paper.
3. Place whole grain tortilla on pizza pan and bake for 7 - 9 minutes or until crispy and golden brown.
4. Let cool.
5. Spread a layer of hummus and add toppings of your choice.
6. Put back in oven for 7-10 minutes or just enough to heat up toppings.
7. Top with nutritional yeast and serve. Enjoy!

Chickpea Salad Sandwich

Ingredients:

- 3 - 14 oz can of chickpeas
- 1 avocado
- 2 ribs of celery, chopped
- ⅓ c fresh dill, minced
- 1 red onion, chopped
- 1 c fresh parsley
- 3 Tablespoons lemon juice
- ½ tsp. salt
- ½ tsp. ground pepper
- Vegan bread
- Sriracha (optional)

Instructions:

1. Add chickpeas & avocado to a large bowl and mash until mostly smooth.
2. Mix in celery, dill, red onion, lemon juice, salt and ground pepper.
3. Once mixed serve mixture on two slices of bread to make a sandwich or chill for later.
4. Top with sriracha, which is optional.

Mexican Avocado Salad

Ingredients:

- 24 cherry tomatoes, sliced in quarters
- 2 tbsp. extra virgin olive oil
- 4 tsp. red wine vinegar
- 1 tsp. salt
- ¼ tsp. ground pepper
- ½ red onion, finely chopped
- 2 tbsp. fresh cilantro

- 2 Avocados
- 1 - 15 oz can black beans
- 1 - 15 oz yellow corn or 1 c frozen corn
- Organic spring mix lettuce

Instructions:

1. Heat corn in a small saucepan until warm and tender.
2. Heat black beans in a small saucepan until warm and tender.
3. Drain juices from black beans and corn. Set aside in a large bowl.
4. Add tomatoes, olive oil, vinegar, salt, and pepper to large bowl with vegetables. Stir and let sit for 30 minutes to an hour at room temperature.
5. Add onion and cilantro to the large bowl after it has sat for 30 minutes to an hour. Stir.
6. Arrange your favorite lettuce mix on a plate and top with mixture then top with avocado.
7. Grab a fork and enjoy!

Black Bean & Corn Burgers

Ingredients:

- 2 - 15 oz can of black beans
- ½ c of frozen corn (thawed)
- ½ yellow onion, diced
- 3 tsp. ketchup
- 1 1/2 tsp. yellow mustard
- 2 tsp. garlic powder
- ¾ c quick oats

Instructions:

1. Preheat oven to 400 degrees F.

2. Grease cookie sheet or line with parchment paper and set aside

3. Drain and rinse black beans and put into a large mixing bowl.

4. Mash beans until pureed.

5. Stir in corn, onion, ketchup, mustard, garlic powder and oats. If mixture seems to dry to form patties add more ketchup.

6. Form patties and put on cookie sheet.

7. Bake for 10 minutes then flip over to bake for another 5-7 minutes.

8. Once done put patty on a Vegan bun and serve with your favorite toppings such as lettuce, tomatoes, etc. Enjoy!

Easy Curried Quinoa Salad

Ingredients:

- ½ c quinoa
- 1 c organic vegetable broth
- 1 tsp. yellow curry powder
- 4 c organic spring mix salad
- ½ c raisins
- Cilantro minced to add as garnish
- Braggs Aminos for dressing (optional)

Instructions:

1. Wash and strain quinoa. Place quinoa in a saucepan with broth, curry powder, paprika. Bring to a boil.

2. Once boiling cover and reduce heat to a low simmer for 15 minutes or until juices have evaporated.

3. Stir in raisins once sauce pan has been removed from stove.

4. Place salad mix on a plate and add quinoa topping and garnish with cilantro.

5. Add Braggs Aminos for dressing or your favorite dressing.

6. Grab a fork and enjoy!

Vietnamese Spring Rolls

Ingredients:

- 1 package thin rice noodles
- 1 head of lettuce chopped
- 1 bag of matchstick carrots
- 2 cucumbers sliced into matchsticks
- 1 c fresh mint thinly sliced
- 2 packages of tofu, sliced (we use Wildwood Teriyaki)
- Olive oil
- 1 package spring roll wrappers / rice paper
- Coconut Aminos by Coconut Secrets (or your favorite dipping sauce)

Instructions:

1. Heat olive oil in a pan on medium heat. Lightly brown tofu on both sides. Set aside.
2. Cook rice noodles according to instructions. Set aside when done.
3. Set out ingredients in individual bowls in an assembly line.
4. Grab a large pan to soak rice paper one at a time. Once rice paper is soft lay out on a hard surface such as a cutting board.
5. Add a small handful of rice noodle towards one end, carrots, lettuce, mint, and tofu.
6. Roll spring roll up according to instructions on the wrapper.
7. Keep on rolling until all ingredients or wrappers are gone.
8. Dip in your favorite dipping sauce. Enjoy!

Dinner Recipes

Minestrone Soup

Ingredients:

- 2 medium potatoes cut into cubes
- 2 large carrots chopped into half moons
- 1 medium onion chopped
- 2 garlic cloves chopped
- 3 stalks of celery chopped
- 1 zucchini cut into half moons
- ½ c of uncooked lentils
- 1 - 14 oz can of crushed tomatoes
- ½ c small shell pasta
- 4 c cabbage shredded
- 7 cups vegetable broth
- ½ c minced fresh basil
- ½ c chopped fresh parsley

Salt and pepper to taste

Instructions:

1. Heat oil on medium heat in a large soup pot. Add carrots, zucchini, onion, celery and sauté for 3-5 minutes until onions start to appear soft and brown.
2. Add potato and garlic and cook for another minute.
3. Add diced tomatoes, washed lentils and cook for another 30 seconds or so.
4. Pour broth into soup pot and bring to a simmer.
5. Cook until potatoes become tender.
6. Add pasta, a pinch of salt & pepper and cabbage. Keep simmering for about 5-10 minutes until pasta is done.
7. Once done remove from heat. Season with salt and pepper to your liking and serve up in a bowl.
8. Garnish with parsley and fresh basil.
9. Grab a spoon and enjoy!

Easy Spaghetti & Meatless Meatballs

Ingredients:

• 2 bags of frozen meatless meatballs or meatless crumbles (beyond meat or Gardein)
• 1 - 24 oz jar of your favorite organic spaghetti sauce
• 1 c tomato sauce
• 2 tbsp. fresh oregano
• 2 tbsp. fresh basil
• 1 tsp. garlic powder
• 4 tbsp. organic brown sugar
• 1 box of organic spaghetti
• Nutritional Yeast

Instructions:

1. Cook spaghetti in boiling water until done.
2. While spaghetti is cooking mix together in a large saucepan, spaghetti sauce, meatless meatballs, tomato sauce, oregano, basil, garlic powder, brown sugar. Heat ingredients on medium low heat to a simmer. Stir often.
3. Once meatless meatballs are done and spaghetti is cooked mix together in a large bowl.
4. Serve and top with nutritional yeast. Enjoy!

Veggie Spice Fried Rice

Ingredients:

- 2 tsp. olive oil
- ½ yellow onion, chopped
- 2 carrots chopped
- ¼ tsp. Chinese 5 spice powder
- 2 garlic cloves, minced
- 1 ½ tbsp. tamari
- 1 tbsp. rice wine vinegar
- 1 tsp. chili paste or sriracha
- 4 cups cooked short grain rice
- 1 c spinach, chopped
- ½ c green onions
- 1 package frozen mixed vegetables (thawed)
- 1 package tofu (we use a flavored one from Wildwood)

Instructions:

1. Cook rice in a rice cooker and set aside when done.
2. In a large wok heat oil over medium heat. Add onions, tofu, and carrots and cook until onions are translucent.
3. Add 5 spice powder, garlic, mix well, then remove from pan and set aside.

4. In a small glass bowl mix tamari sauce, vinegar, chili paste or sriracha.
5. Add oil to wok if needed and heat up to medium heat.
6. Add rice and stir until it's warm.
7. Drizzled sauce over rice and stir.
8. Stir in onion, carrots, mixed vegetables and stir fry until warm. About 1 - 2 minutes.
9. Fold in spinach and green onions. Serve immediately and enjoy!

Vegan Lentil Tacos

Ingredients:

- 1 c of dried brown lentils (save time if you want and use canned lentils)
- 8 oz. can of tomato sauce
- 1 packet of taco seasoning mix (Vegan)
- ¼ c water
- Corn tortillas
- Vegan shredded cheese (We use Daiya)
- Romaine lettuce shredded
- ¼ c chopped cilantro
- 1 tomato diced
- Salsa
- Avocado, sliced

Instructions:

1. Soak the lentils in a large glass bowl until soft, about one hour (unless you are using canned lentils skip and just transfer to saucepan).
2. Put lentils in a saucepan and mix with tomato sauce and taco seasoning. Add about ¼ cup of water. Simmer on low until heated.
3. Spoon mixture into corn tortillas.

4. Top with romaine lettuce, cilantro, salsa, diced tomatoes, avocado slices and Vegan shredded cheese. Enjoy!

Black Bean Burritos

Ingredients:

- 2 cups cooked rice
- 2 - 14 oz black beans
- 1 chopped onion
- 2 tbsp. olive oil
- 1 c chopped cilantro
- 1 diced tomato
- 1 c frozen corn
- Salsa
- Avocado
- Vegan wheat tortillas (any flavor will do just make sure it's Vegan)

Instructions:

1. Finely chop cilantro and cook ½ c of the cilantro with your rice in a rice cooker. Save the other ½ c for later.
2. Sauté onions over medium heat with olive oil until lightly brown and translucent. Set aside
3. Cook black beans and corn over medium low heat just enough to simmer and warm the vegetables.
4. Drain juices from vegetables.
5. Put vegetables in a medium glass bowl. Mix in onions and diced tomatoes.
6. Warm tortilla up in microwave for about 15 seconds depending on the power of the microwave times may vary.
7. Add vegetable mixture to tortilla and top with salsa, cilantro and avocado.
8. Wrap up like a burrito and enjoy!

Loaded Nachos

Ingredients:

- ½ bag of tortilla chips (we use Beanitos)
- ½ c. chopped tomatoes
- ¼ c finely chopped red onion
- ½ c black beans
- 1 c Vegan cheddar cheese (we use Daiya)
- 1 finely chopped jalapeno (optional)
- ½ c - 1 c. shredded lettuce
- Salsa
- ½ c. guacamole (mashed avocado, lime juice, pinch of salt)

Instructions:

1. Preheat oven to 425 degrees.
2. Spread chips evenly across baking pan.
3. Top with black beans, jalapeno, onion, and cheese.
4. Bake 5-7 minutes.
5. Turn oven to broil and cook for another 2-3 minutes until cheese melts.
6. Top with shredded lettuce, salsa and guacamole. Enjoy!

Mexican Casserole

Ingredients:

Mexican Blend
- 1 tbsp. chili powder
- 1 ½ tsp. ground cumin
- ½ tsp. paprika
- ¼ tsp. cayenne pepper

- 1 ¼ tsp. Himalayan salt

Casserole
- 2 tsp. olive oil
- 1 red onion, diced
- 3 garlic cloves, minced
- 1 green bell pepper
- 1 red bell pepper
- 1 yellow bell pepper
- 1 jalapeno seeded and diced
- Salt & Pepper
- 1 c frozen corn
- 1 - 14 oz can diced tomatoes
- 1 c tomato sauce
- 3 cups chopped spinach
- 1 - 15 oz can of black beans
- 1 box of spiral pasta
- 1 Vegan shredded cheese (we use Daiya)
- 2 - 3 handfuls of crushed tortilla chips
- 1 - 2 avocados

Instructions:

1. Make Mexican blend. In a small glass bowl, mix together chili powder, cumin, paprika, cayenne pepper and salt.
2. Bring water to a boil in a large pot. Add pasta and cook until done. Drain and set aside.
3. Make casserole by first pre-heating oven to 375 degrees F.

4. While boiling pasta, in a large wok, heat oil over medium heat. Add onion, garlic, bell peppers, jalapeno and sauté for 10 minutes until softened. Season with salt and pepper.

5. Stir in Mexican blend, corn, diced tomatoes with juices, tomato sauce, spinach, beans, and add ½ cup of Vegan cheese. Season with more salt and pepper if needed.

6. Pour mixture into a large casserole dish. Sprinkle top of casserole with remaining cheese and crushed chips. Cover with tin foil and bake for 15 minutes.

7. After 15 minutes uncover and cook for an additional 10 minutes

8. Remove from oven and scoop out portions into a bowl and top with sliced or cubed avocados.

9. Grab a fork and enjoy!

Bold Flavor Sloppy Joes

Ingredients:

*   1 tbsp. plus 1 teaspoon olive oil, divided
*   1 medium onion, diced medium
*   1 pound seitan, chopped into small pieces
*   3 cloves garlic, minced
*   1 tbsp. minced fresh ginger
*   2 tbsp. chopped fresh thyme
*   1 tbsp. sweet paprika
*   1/2 tsp. salt
*   1/2 tsp. allspice
*   1/2 tsp. crushed red pepper flakes
*   1/8 tsp. cinnamon
*   Vegan buns

Instructions:

1. Preheat a large pan over medium-high heat. Add onion and sauté with one tablespoon olive oil and a pinch of salt, until translucent, 3 to 5 minutes.
2. Add the seitan, stir and cook for about 10 minutes, stirring often. Add garlic and ginger and continue to sauté for 1 -2 more minutes. Add remaining olive oil.
3. Add thyme, paprika, salt, allspice, red pepper flakes, cinnamon and black pepper to seitan mixture. Stir well.
4. Add the tomatoes, and cook for about 10 more minutes, stirring and turning over often.
5. Mix in the maple syrup, lime juice and mustard. Cook for a minute or so, then taste for salt and seasonings, and serve on a toasted Vegan bun. Enjoy!

Vegetable Fettuccini

Ingredients:

- 1 medium cauliflower
- ½ tsp. extra virgin olive oil
- 1 tbsp. minced garlic
- ½ c unsweetened almond milk
- ¼ c nutritional yeast
- 1 tbsp. fresh lemon juice
- ½ tsp. garlic powder
- ¾ tsp. Himalayan salt
- ¼ tsp. pepper
- 1 - 8 oz box of fettuccine
- 1 bag of frozen mixed vegetables (taken out of freezer at the start of recipe)

Instructions:

1. Add cauliflower florets to a large pot and cover with water. Bring to a boil and cook until tender. About 5-7 minutes. Drain water from cauliflower and add to a food processor or Vitamix.
2. While cauliflower is cooking sauté in a medium pan garlic over low heat until softened.
3. Add sautéed garlic to Vitamix or food processor with milk, nutritional yeast, lemon juice, garlic powder, salt and pepper. Blend on high until smooth. Add water to change consistency if too thick.
4. Add pasta to a large pot of boiling water and cook according to package instructions. Drain and add back to large pot.
5. Add cauliflower sauce, frozen vegetables to pasta and heat over medium heat stirring regularly until veggies are heated.
6. Salt and pepper to taste and enjoy!

Pad Thai

Ingredients:

Sauce
- 4 tbsp. peanut butter
- Juice of 4 limes
- 4 tbsp. cane sugar
- Sriracha to taste

Noodles
- 14 oz rice noodles
- 1 frozen bag of broccoli florets
- 4 garlic cloves
- ½ c shredded carrots
- 1 cup of sliced green onions
- ¼ c cilantro, chopped

- 2 tsp. olive oil
- 2 packages of tofu (we use wildwood sprouted tofu)

Additional Toppings:
- ½ c chopped peanuts
- 2 limes cut into wedges
- 1 c of sprouts (choose your favorite)
- 1 - 2 cups shredded cabbage

Instructions:

1. Cut tofu into bite sized pieces.
2. Heat medium sauce pan with olive oil. Place bite sized tofu pieces in pan and cook just enough to lightly brown. Set aside.
3. In a large pot cook pasta according to instructions on package. When done, drain and set aside.
4. Mix together peanut butter, juice of limes and cane sugar in a small glass bowl. Add desired amount of sriracha.
5. Heat oil in a large pan or wok over medium heat. When pan is hot, sauté garlic and broccoli & carrots, sauté until tender. Add more oil if needed.
6. Stir in tofu, noodles and sauce. Cook for another minute.
7. Fold in green onions and cilantro.
8. Serve while warm and top with peanuts, lime juice from wedges and cabbage.

Megan Alpha

From My Kitchen to Yours,

Thank you for purchase and taking time to read through this eBook. I hope you enjoyed all the suggestions, tips and recipes. Wherever you are in your Vegan journey I am here to support you. Feel free to join our very active community over on my social media channels:

- *Facebook*
- *Instagram*
- *Twitter*
- *YouTube*
- *My Vegan Dreams Blog*

Here's a little bit more about me:

Just in case you missed it, my name is Megan Alpha and as of 2017 I am an 18 year old Vegan who has committed to the Vegan lifestyle.

I made the decision to go Vegan back in August of 2014, when my mom and I were on a family vacation in New Hampshire. We had just got done eating dinner and something weird occurred to me.

People were devouring their meals and commenting openly about how amazing the lobster tasted, the fish, the beef; and for some reason I became disgusted. Literally sick to my stomach.

That night my mom and I started to research how lobsters were caught and killed, which horrified me. I had no idea their entire bodies were made up of nerves and they could feel everything.

I thought to myself how selfish I was for killing a living being just to satisfy my taste buds.

That thought led me to research and start watching videos on the process of how chickens, cows, lambs, fish, pigs, ducks, buffalo, calves and egg products made it to our dinner plates.

I was horrified.

I realized at that very moment I could no longer participate in such cruelty to animals.

I went VEGAN cold turkey with my mother. I will admit it did take a month or so to really educated myself on what is Vegan and what it is not when it comes to prepared meals and eating out.

Now, being Vegan is easy for me. It's not only about what I put in my body but what I also put on my body.

It's not about being Vegan for me, it's a lifestyle.

My goal and mission is to inspire and educate young and old on how to become Vegan and how to deal with the issues that arise from being Vegan. Such as what to eat when one goes out, how to deal with unsporting family members, how to respond to questions people ask about being Vegan and much, much more...

I want to be a voice for our animals who don't have a voice.

It's my dream that one day the majority of our society will realize that Vegan is the way to go.

It's good for you, the environment, and most of all the animals. Ultimately, I want to educate as many people as I can around the world.

Here's to being VEGAN! Ⓥ Megan the Vegan! Ⓥ

For the Animals, the Environment, and the People

Printed in Great Britain
by Amazon